SINK OR SWIM

HOW MY FAMILY AND I MET GOD IN THE MIDDLE OF THE OCEAN

Eric Tolbert

You can visit our website at www.SinkOrSwimBook.com.

Eric Tolbert
P.O. Box 4036
Battle Creek MI 49016

Cover Design By Nick Stokes Photography

Author Photo By Doug Johnson

Sister Janice,

Thank you for your love &
Support throughout the years!
You mean a great deal to
My family & I. We love you
& Pray Gods blessings & favor
Continue to follow you.

"Always remember, with God
You can Survive Every Storm"

Joshua 1:9

Sink Or Swim

CONTENTS

A Letter I Received From My Father

Eric,

I enjoyed your visit the last time you and the family were down. Your boys are growing up and I 'm very proud of all of them. They are all going to be very successful as young men when they grow up because of you and Freda and prayers. We are praying the Lord puts His covering over them and make them mighty men in the Lord. And speaking of Freda I am so proud of my Daughter in Law. She is so talented and she fits into the family like apples in an apple pie, or better yet like chips in a Freda Lay bag. Smile! (That's where I got the name Chips from) And of course I'm very proud of you my Son for the many sacrifices you took to become the Pastor of Light House Battle Creek. Many don't know the tireless sacrifices and times you drove back in forth to Battle Creek to service God's people in bad snowy or rainy or sunny weather. Just like the Postman you were faithful to a few but the Lord is going to bless you with many. I'm praying the blessings of Abraham Isaac and Jacob over you and your family.

Oh by the way I wanted to tell you this before I Close

You and Freda's web pages are on the map, they are so professional looking they look better than some of the so called professionals. Keep up the good work keep holding up the high standard of God I wish you Gods speed and many prayers of successful ministry for the Battle Creek Area and the World.

Sincerely,

Dad

03/25/13/11:30 a.m.

Philippians 1:6 (KingJamesVersion)

"Being confident of this very thing, that he which hath begun a good work in you will perform it until the day of Jesus Christ".

A Note From The Author

Due to the fact that this is a memoir, I have tried very carefully and very earnestly to write this book with honesty and with great integrity. It is extremely challenging and difficult to write a book that deals with such sensitive circumstances and difficult events. I realize that no matter how careful a person may attempt to be or how genuine a person's heart may be while penning a memoir, there is always the potential room for someone to become offended. It also becomes easy for the views and the intensions of the writer to be misunderstood and even taken out of context. With that being said, I want to make sure that it is clear from the very beginning, that the motivation and the purpose of writing this book is truly and solely to share our journey with others, so that God can be glorified through every obstacle and every challenge that my family and I have ever had to face and endure. I sincerely and earnestly pray that my heart will truly be felt, and that you will see God clearly as you read through each and every chapter ahead.

In Christ love,

Eric Tolbert

"While wading across the river, a man was caught in a powerful undertow. He cried out, Lord I'm afraid. The Lord answered, Fear not, I am your refuge and strength, trust me. So the drowning man pleaded, Lord I am weak I cannot make it on my own. Again the Lord responded, in your weakness I am strong, trust me. Suddenly, the current shifted and the man was swept to shore. He shouted his gratitude to the heavens. Thank you Lord... I am stronger, I'm wiser, I'm better, I never would have made it without you. You are my God."

-Reverend Jesse Jackson

This is an introduction given by Reverend Jackson to introduce the song Never Would Have Made It, at BET's Celebration of Gospel.

Sink Or Swim

INTRODUCTION

A couple of years ago after writing in my journal, I made a decision to write out and record the journey that my family and I had to go through to get to where we are today. It is an amazing journey filled with laughter, extreme faith, and a whole lot of pain and tears. I have tried on many occasions to pen this journey however, it has been painful reliving some of our more hard pressing moments. This time around, I determined within myself to stay focused and to record both the joys and the pains of what my family and I have had to endure. It was not my original intent for what started off as journaling to evolve into the book you have today. But after looking and reading back throughout our journey and discovering such an amazing testament of God's provision, protection, and purpose - it was impossible to keep this journey to ourselves. What you are reading now is not just a memoir of a moment in our life, but I strongly believe that this book will also become a source of strength to so many people who may be enduring some hard pressing issues of their own. My hope is that in the

1

same way journaling our story on paper has become a means of restoration and healing for myself, that reading our story will equally provide encouragement and inspiration to every person who travels through its pages.

This book carries aspects of my life that until now, only few people have known about. Not even my own congregation is aware of many of the challenges that their Pastor and First Family have had to face and endure. With that being said, I want to make sure that it is emphatically clear that I did not write this book to demoralize or to put anyone down. This book was not at all written as a backlash or as a means to slander. I wrote this book solely and completely as a testimony of God's amazing keeping power. Throughout the last several years, God has without question revealed to my family and I, that He is indeed Jehovah-Jirah, the God who provides. The only thing about sharing a personal testimony is that in order to truly express what God has done in your life, sometimes the most painful areas of our lives must be exposed. I have wrestled many days and nights, trying my best to discover ways to express our testimony without having to reveal some of our most painful moments. Besides, it would seem that just simply knowing that God has in some way delivered my family and I from "*something,*" would be powerful enough in itself. The only problem that I have discovered with that thought, is the fact that labeling God's miracles as just *"something He brought you out of,"* does God such a great disservice. It brings so much more glory to a masterful Creator, when you are able to reveal the journey that He has protected, provided, and guided you through. It is then that people are able to clearly see what God has truly delivered you from, and give all glory to where the glory is truly deserved. I suppose the Genesis account of the story of Joseph would have still been impactful had it simply shared with us Joseph's dream, and then taken us directly from his pillow to the palace - revealing to us only the very end of his journey. With no hint of uncertainty, it would have still clearly affirmed that God had done exactly what He had revealed to Joseph that He was going to do. But if that would have happened, as great as it would have been to simply know that God was able to keep His promise, we would have never seen how God was able to keep Joseph through the process. We would have completely missed the hand of God covering Joseph through betrayal, protecting Joseph while in slavery, giving Joseph strength while being tempted, keeping Joseph through painful lies, preserving Joseph while in prison, and then finally promoting Joseph into his place of purpose and destiny. Every stage and every obstacle that Joseph had to face was significantly important, as it renders more and more glory to a mighty God while his story is unraveled throughout the scriptures. What I have written in this book has only been unveiled, so that when you finally get to the end, you will see clearly that the only person that can get the glory out of every obstacle that we have ever had to face, is God alone. Not myself, not my family, nor anyone else.... only God.

My sincere prayer is that as you read this book, that God will arise to the forefront of every page. My heart's desire is that in some way, our personal journey will not only become a means of encouragement to you, but that it will also push and propel you to trust and believe God in ways that you have never done before. So as you now get on board this boat that will soon be leaving this dock to travel back to where my family and I encountered God, please watch your step, keep your life jackets fastened and secure. I guarantee you, the course will get boisterous at times, but at the end of the journey, my prayer is that you will see, experience, and discover God in the same ways that our family did back then. If you are ready, let the journey now begin.

Sink Or Swim

CHAPTER ONE

ALL ABOARD

When publically acknowledged by Pastor Marvin Sapp and introduced as the Senior Pastor of one of his Lighthouse church locations, he generally would openly express to the crowd that there was a time in which he told my family and I, "Now you must either sink or swim." Sitting on the front row as what would appear to be skilled swimming survivors who have now safely and easily made it back to shore, my mind always travels back to the very moments that he is referring to. Both my wife and I graciously smile as we glance across the audience. We realize that everyone in the room is absolutely oblivious as to what those three words "Sink or Swim" really means, until now. In the next few chapters, I want to share with you how my family and I met God in the middle of the ocean.

I remember when my wife and I first joined Lighthouse. The church was meeting at a multi-purpose center and there was such a buzz about the ministry that was sweeping throughout the city. When my wife and I came to visit the church for the very first time, we had such an amazing experience. It was hard to believe that this church had just recently opened as the ministry was packed with people from the front to the back. Everyone was so cordial and friendly, and the freedom to worship was exactly what my family and I was looking for.

Before we had first visited the Lighthouse church, I had just come from helping a Pastor friend of mine out with his church. He was in need of a musician and he had asked me to come help assist his church in that area, and I agreed. I had a great time working with his church and their praise team. The Pastor and First Lady of that church were and are still great, humble, genuine and very kind hearted people. Their music ministry was blessed with very gifted and anointed young women of God that would always sing with such passion and fire for the Lord. God would surely visit us in those services. Along with helping their church out with their music ministry, I was also able to help assist them with their youth ministry as well.

The Pastor of that church began going through some challenging times, and because of an unexpected and an unavoidable circumstance, for a season he asked me to step in and take over as the Pastor of his congregation. I will never forget the day that his wife called and shared her husband's desire for me to take over their church for a season. *Me?*, I thought to myself. *You want me to take over the church?* I didn't know the first thing about being a Pastor or even what the responsibilities of being a Pastor really entailed. After speaking with his wife over the phone and

6

praying about it, I made a decision to help the church out as best as I could. There were so many questions racing through my head that day, *How will the people respond to this situation? Will they even be willing to accept me as their temporary leader?*

In my early moments of taking over as the Pastor of that ministry, one afternoon I remember driving up to the church to begin preparing for a bible study that would be taking place later on that evening. I knew that in a few hours I would be standing in front of a congregation that would be anticipating receiving a word from the Lord. As I walked up to the church building getting ready to enter, I was presented with one of my very first gifts as being the new Pastor. I was graciously greeted by an eviction notice that was posted at the front entrance. What was I suppose to do now? Not only had this ministry unexpectedly received a new young Pastor, but they had also just lost their place of worship as well.

I was twenty-five years old at the time and I had to quickly determine what the next moves for this ministry needed to be. As I prayed, God began to guide and direct my steps, and I found myself at a nearby hotel that was willing to rent a small conference room out to us for an affordable price. We moved the church services to that location temporarily, and as we began to pray and follow God's direction, things began to turn around for the ministry. That was my first encounter ever with the office of a Senior Pastor. I had been a Youth Pastor before, but I would have never imagined myself carrying out the responsibilities of being a Shepherd over an entire flock, especially during that season of my life.

Though the Pastor did return back briefly for a moment, and then once again stepped away because of his situation, I helped to pastor that congregation altogether for roughly a year's time. After that, my friend returned back and completely regained the pastorate over his church. He is still a good friend, and he is working strongly and passionately toward advancing God's kingdom to this very day. That one year undoubtedly taught me more about ministry than I could have ever imagine however, there was still so much more to be learned. I was entrusted to take over a church that was going through some difficult challenges. To some, it may have seemed much easier to simply walk away and move forward with my own life. I was married to a beautiful woman, I had a young son, and I was also working another job to take care of my family as their church was not in a financial position to be able to bless us monetarily. But for some reason, I could not walk away.

There is an important truth that we must learn concerning the kingdom. A truth that seems to be slowly fading away within the realm of popular church culture. The truth is that ministry is not all about what we can get or receive, but that ministry is truly about what we can give to others. I have discovered that when you genuinely serve others with the right heart and spirit, God honors that, and He will bless those who are a blessing to others. Luke 6:38 says, *Give, and it shall be given unto you; good*

8

measure, pressed down, and shaken together, and running over, shall men give into your bosom. Most people stop there without reading further, but that same verse says, *For with the same measure that ye mete withal it shall be measured to you again.* I love the way The New Living Translation writes it. It says, *The amount you give, will determine the amount you get back.* We must return back to the place where our greatest reward does not come from being the recipient of being served, but where our greatest reward comes from serving others, even if at times it may be a sacrifice on our end. And though there is a reward that will return to those who give with the right heart and with the right spirit, our greatest joy should always be in knowing that we were able to be a blessing to someone else.

When I accepted the assignment to help pastor my friend's church, I thought that I was simply doing him a favor. I was standing in the gap, helping a friend to keep his church in operation until he was able to fully return. Little did I know that God was strategically setting the stage and preparing me for something greater in my future.

After I turned the church back over to its original Pastor, my wife and I began the quest and the search to find a church home for our family. We had visited a few churches, and I had even briefly helped another church out with their music ministry. But once we had discovered the new Lighthouse church, we knew that Lighthouse was our home. Having been a pastor over a church for a small period of time was also another reason why our visits to Lighthouse were so revitalizing. It was just simply refreshing to be able to come, sit down, and participate in worship without having the weight and the responsibilities of an entire ministry resting on my shoulders.

Though our worship experience at Lighthouse was something new to us, our relationship with Pastor Marvin and Pastor MaLinda was not. In fact several years prior, at one point we all attended the same church together. The church that we attended together back then, is a church that carries an extremely rich legacy in the city of Grand Rapids Michigan even now. Still to this day, it is a church that remains strong and is under great leadership as it continues to be a thriving and a very progressive church. The Pastor of that church at the time we all attended, was a great man of God who inspired and poured into the lives of many prominent Bishops, Pastors, leaders, musicians, and even singers who are notably recognized around the globe. Many of the individuals in whom he has poured into and personally encouraged throughout the years are considered to be major influential pillars in the body of Christ even to this very day.

When my wife and I attended that church, Pastor Marvin was the Youth Pastor at the time. I had a friend who worked closely with Pastor Marvin on his youth board, and he was also the Director over a youth organization that I was volunteering with at the time. It was through him that I was introduced to the church's youth ministry and also introduced to Pastor Marvin as well. Shortly thereafter, my wife and I became a part of the youth team and we began helping out with the church's youth services, events, and activities.

Pastor Marvin's solo career was beginning to expand. Between his music ministry and his evangelistic ministry, even back then his schedule could prove to be a bit taxing at times. When Pastor Marvin was in town, he would speak during the youth services himself, but if he was on the road and unable to attend, there were a few hand selected people that he would entrust to speak to the young people in his absence. Somehow I became one of those individuals that he would entrust to share with the youth while he was gone. Though my wife and I were a part of the youth board, and though I had an opportunity to speak for Pastor Marvin on several occasions, we really only knew of each other from small interactions during youth board meetings or through brief interactions at the youth services. Just as my wife and I were beginning to get more involved with the youth ministry at that church, that is when my Pastor friend requested for me to assist him with his church. So when my wife and I later came to visit the newly launched Lighthouse Church, because we had worked together before, we knew of Pastor Marvin and Pastor MaLinda, and they also knew of us.

JOINING LIGHTHOUSE CHURCH

I'll never forget before officially joining Lighthouse, after an evening bible study, my wife and I had an opportunity to sit down and talk with Pastor Marvin. It was a very brief conversation, and I remember sharing with him some of the things that we had just experienced from helping out the previous church we had attended. I remember telling him how I looked forward to being able to sit and be refreshed under his ministry. During that meeting, Pastor Marvin was very respectful, receptive, and very courteous. I remember leaving the church that night feeling like a huge burden had been lifted up off of me. We had connected to a place where my family and I could be encouraged, empowered, strengthened and now even grow together. Most importantly, I was glad that we had found a place that we could now call home.

After joining Lighthouse, for two years my wife and I focused on simply receiving the word of God. We rested up while getting spiritually rejuvenated and we greatly enjoyed our time of being refilled. We would come to service, receive the word of God, and graciously make our way right back to our car once the services had concluded. It was a much needed time of refreshing for the both of us. Those first two years at Lighthouse were also important to me because I wanted to show my faithfulness and commitment to the ministry. I wanted it to be undoubtedly clear that I was not joining the ministry because of who Pastor Marvin was, or because I was trying to receive a position from "the new church in town." I wanted it to be clear that I had joined the church simply because I felt led by God that Lighthouse was the place where my family and I needed to be. After two years of sitting and being refreshed, I was now ready to start getting involved with the ministry. The church had moved from having their services at a multipurpose center, to now having their services at a church building that they were purchasing. The ministry was growing and thriving fast, and the more the church grew, the greater the need was for volunteers and helpers to serve in the ministry.

When expressing my willingness to start getting involved with the church, I envisioned myself starting off as a Brother Servant. A Brother Servant is a person who does anything from ushering people to their seats, to assisting and helping around the church with anything that may be needed. I grew up in a church environment where we would see predominately women serving in areas like ushering, and there was absolutely nothing wrong with that. But at Lighthouse, the men led in serving, which allowed our sisters to be able to enjoy the services. Seeing men in position impacted me greatly, and it is something that I will never forget. I imagined myself wearing one of those black suits with the gold ties that all the Brother Servants wore. Needless to say, that year I did not become a Brother Servant, but that year Pastor Marvin and Pastor MaLinda announced that I would be the new leader over their high school youth ministry.

APPOINTED AS THE LEADER OVER THE HIGH SCHOOL YOUTH

I remember the day when we found out that I had been selected to be the leader over the high school ministry. Every year Pastor Marvin and Pastor MaLinda would have a special service where they would announce to the congregation who would be leading for that upcoming year. Some leaders that were announced may be new leaders appointed into position, others may be the same leaders who held that office the previous year before, but every year leadership positions where subject to change. That night my wife and I had no idea that we were going to be announced as the new leaders over the high school youth ministry. When the announcement was made we were completely shocked, but at the same time we were extremely excited for such an opportunity.

When our names were called that night, we walked up to the front of the church and stood next to all of the other individuals who had been appointed into leadership positions for that year. I remember having such a feeling of excitement as I was humbled and honored to have even been considered for the position. As the final person who was selected to be a leader for that year joined the rest of the team up front, the church gave us all a roaring standing ovation. It was a completely overwhelming moment.

As I stood there in front of the congregation overlooking the crowd, I felt God impress in my spirit these words. He said to me, "Get ready for the journey." At that time I had no idea what those words meant, or even why God would impress those words into my spirit. All I knew was that God was telling me to get ready for something, and whether good or bad I was soon about to discover what it was.

REBUILDING THE HIGH SCHOOL YOUTH DEPARTMENT

When I took over the high school youth ministry, there were many young people who were disconnected and no longer engaged. I remember going up to the classrooms to watch what was taking place in the youth department before taking over as the high school leader. I noticed that some students would remain downstairs in the regular services opposed to even coming up to be a part of their youth classes. For many of the youth, their relationship with Christ was almost non-existent, and many lacked an understanding and a knowledge of the scriptures. At one point, the teachers had been instructed to take the entire youth ministry through a curriculum that taught the "basics of the bible," as many of the older students were unable to answer what would seem to be simplistic Sunday School questions. Unfortunately, when the young people were being taught about God and the bible, there were many who had little interest to even learn about those things. It is because a desire for God and His word can only be ignited through a true relationship with Him from within. Without it, it's like trying to light a fire on a gas stove that has no gas in it. Yes your purpose may be to produce fire, but you must have inside of you what is needed to burn. Unfortunately, the majority of the high school youth at that time did not have that kind of relationship with God, so there was no drive or any true passion to learn more about God or about His word.

Observing the youths condition, I began to pray and seek God for direction as to how we could take the high school youth ministry to another level. It is important to note that I am a man of order. I have always believed strongly in submitting to the authority of those who lead over you. There are many leaders who have amazing skills, outstanding gifts, and limitless ambitions however, their greatest downfall lies in their inability to submit properly to authority. It was important to me that anything that I put into action first received the permission and approval of Pastor Marvin and Pastor MaLinda. I would put together proposals with any thoughts or ideals that I had for the high school youth, and then submit the proposals to them for their review. Everything was contingent upon their decision of whether to move forward with it or not.

After observing the condition of the youth and praying about the best approach to take concerning the high school ministry, I put together a proposal that laid out some things that I believed could help jump start the youth. After Pastor Marvin and Pastor MaLinda reviewed the proposal, they approved for me to proceed forward. I immediately began to do things to try and cultivate the youth's attention in an attempt to bring them back into the classroom body, mind, and spirit. The goal was to try and give them more of a desire to find out about who Christ really was. We tried to teach them the word of God in a relevant, engaging, and practical kind of way. We met with the youth on Sundays as well as on Tuesday evenings during regular bible study. On selected bible class nights, we would load up the church van and take the youth out to a nice Café to discuss the word of God over Latte's and Hot Chocolate. The youth loved it, and as we began to incorporate the same message with a different approach, the high school ministry began to grow and flourish. Our class sessions went from being lower in attendance to now starting to become overcrowded, and their passion to learn about Christ was deepening.

One thing that I can say about youth ministry is that it is an extreme sacrifice. During those times I would rarely be able to participate in the adult services because my commitment was in making sure that the high school ministry was running smoothly. When we would have revivals and special guest speakers, I seldom got the opportunity to enjoy those services because of having to minister to the youth. Of course all of us who served during those times received a free CD of the services that we had missed however, listening to the CD of a service was never the same. Youth ministry can indeed be a major sacrifice, but it was a sacrifice that I was certainly willing to make.

BEING CONSIDERED AS A FUTURE PASTOR

Every year, Pastor MaLinda would run a mandatory Leadership Course for every person who served in any capacity of ministry at the church. This course was also available for those who may have had an interest or a desire to possibly serve in the ministry at a later time in the future as well. One year in that class, Pastor MaLinda had us all write a paper with an

17

assignment to write out our "Five Year Goals." We were told to explain where we planned to be, and what we planned to be doing in the next five years. In that paper, I began to give a descriptive layout for each of those five years. When I got to the fifth year, I wrote that my desire was to become a Senior Pastor over a church, and that my wife and I desired to start a church ministry in Portland Oregon. Some years earlier when I was first hired into my job, my wife and I were sent to Portland Oregon for three weeks to receive new staff training. After being in Portland for nearly a month, we immediately fell in love with the place. When we returned home from training that year, my wife and I began talking about how much we felt a connection to that city. From that day forward, we truly believed that one day we would start a church in Portland Oregon. We had a name for our ministry already picked out and everything. It was going to be called Living Water Worship Center.

After sharing that information in my leadership report, it was not too much later that my wife and I found ourselves sitting in Pastor Marvin's office talking with him and Pastor MaLinda. I remember them encouraging my wife and I and advising us that they too recognized the call of a Pastor on our lives. They told us that God had placed it on their heart to properly set up individuals in ministry to help them be able to walk out their calling. They shared with us a few details of their own personal journey that they had to endure in order to start the Lighthouse church. It was through those challenges that a passion was birthed in them to help others to be launched

18

out successfully. They told us that they had made a promise to themselves, that when they sent out sons and daughters in the ministry, that they were going to make sure that none of them would ever have to go through the same things that they went through in order to get started. They then advised us that they were considering and strongly praying about possibly sending us out as Pastors one day in the future. My wife and I sat in their office absolutely amazed.

After leaving that meeting, there was an overwhelming feeling of gratitude, joy, and excitement that had come over us. I was grateful toward God for this season of my life. Everything seemed to be falling into right alignment. I was married to a beautiful woman, I was in good health, I now had two amazing sons, I was working for an internationally recognized youth ministry getting paid to do what I already loved to do (which was mentor and minister to young people). I had food in my refrigerator, great health insurance, I was over my church's high school youth ministry, and I had just left a meeting with Pastor Marvin & Pastor MaLinda Sapp being told that they were considering possibly sending me out as a Pastor in the future. Are you kidding me? This "Journey" that God was telling me to prepare for earlier, was looking promising. With all of these many blessings taking place in our life, what could possibly go wrong?

Sink Or Swim

CHAPTER TWO

RIPPLES OF CONFLICT

While leading our church's high school youth ministry, I was also working for a Para-church youth organization. Para-church ministries are generally Christian ministries or organizations that work separate or outside of the confinements of the local church body. Many of them are interdenominational ministries that have a strong focus on evangelism and outreach. I am not writing this thought as a fact or even as a slight against the church or Para-church organizations, but to me there seems to be a struggle between these two entities effectively working together towards the same common goals. I speak that thought broadly, as there very well may be some areas that have effectively and successfully come together in this wise. This one thing I do know, having worked in a Para-church ministry for nearly seven years, and having been a part of a local church body my entire life, I have discovered that there are many areas in which both of these two entities could really learn and glean from each other.

Though my job responsibilities with the Para-church ministry were geared and focused mainly toward spending time with adolescent youth, there were many other responsibilities that accompanied. There was a lot of traveling as well as a lot of meetings that we were required to attend. From cluster meetings, leadership meetings, regional meetings, committee meetings, to weekend camps and summer camp assignments, there was always something going on.

Our Summer camp assignments would bring us to one of the ministries beautiful camp locations, where our goal was to impact the lives of hundreds of young people who would come from far and wide. Our summer assignments would last anywhere from three to four weeks long, with non-stop activities and ministry being provided for the students and leaders who attended. We would try our very best to make sure that every young person who attended felt as if though camp was just for them. Through the fun, through the beauty of the camp ground itself, through the compassion and servant heart of every volunteer, our hope was that the young people who attended would see God in a new way before finally getting back on their bus or van to return home. Another thing that I loved about summer camp was the fact that our families were allowed to come and stay on the grounds with us during our entire Summer assignment. Having our families present with us seemed to always give us the boost of encouragement needed, helping us to endure the very demanding and challenging responsibilities that our camp assignments could bring.

21

Beyond the frequent meetings that we had to attend and beyond the Winter and Summer camp assignments, there was still a great deal of things that we also needed to accomplish. Many of those responsibilities included, having to develop and manage a leadership team that would spend quality time with young people throughout the school year. We also had to put together and run a weekly program that included games, skits, and the word of God. This description of course does not include doing administrative work or even putting together our two major annual fund-raising events, as well as trying to raise additional funds throughout the year. Then finally came the most important factor of them all. Along with all of these other responsibilities, we ourselves had to personally make sure that we were spending quality time hanging out with the young people that we were trying to reach. Needless to say, there were a lot of things that needed to be done. Balancing my job and volunteering as the head leader over my church's high school youth ministry was a bit challenging, especially considering the times that I would have to go out of town for special meetings or camp assignments. Though balancing these two areas brought about its challenges, they were definitely two areas that I was extremely passionate about, and because of that passion I made the sacrifices necessary to make both of these areas work. I had been employed with my job for the last 6 years, and I had just received a raise and was promoted to now being the Assistant Director over our urban area.

LIGHTHOUSE BATTLE CREEK OPENS

Around this time, Pastor Marvin made a decision to start a second Lighthouse church location. He decided to start the ministry in a city called Battle Creek Michigan. I am told that the reason why Battle Creek was selected, was because there were several individuals living in that city who had heard about the Grand Rapids ministry. They would travel down faithfully to attend the Grand Rapids services. With some encouragement from the individuals who would make a weekly pilgrimage to the Grand Rapids church, Pastor Marvin made a decision to start his second location in the city of Battle Creek. When the second church first opened up, it was amazing. Pastor Marvin and a team from the Grand Rapids church would travel down every Monday night to do what they called "Hour of Power" services. I remember going down to the new Battle Creek Ministry on a couple of occasions and seeing the place overflowing with individuals ready to encounter the Lighthouse experience. At least close to eighty people or more would come out every week on a Monday night to check out this new ministry in town. They started having their services at a building located in downtown Battle Creek. My job also ran a program for young people that took place on Monday evenings as well. That year however, we were delayed in getting our program for the youth started, so this allowed my wife and I to be able to go down and visit the Battle Creek church on occasion.

In addition to now starting a second church location, Pastor Marvin made a decision to go from having two services on Sundays, to now having three services every Sunday at his main church. This decision became a bit of a challenge for some of the areas within the ministry, as they would now have to stretch their volunteers to accommodate the additional service. In fact truthfully speaking, this decision would prove to bring about a level of challenge and taxation on Pastor Marvin himself.

There were many people who after seeing how busy Pastor Marvin had now become, with three services every Sunday at his main location, a brand new church location in an entirely different city which held their services every Monday evening, then a bible study taking place every Tuesday night back home at his main location, not to mention his already tedious and very busy traveling schedule, some began to think that soon Pastor Marvin would have to place someone over the Battle Creek church. There was absolutely no way that he would be able to continue to operate under such taxing and extremely demanding circumstances. There was way too much beginning to pile up on his plate, and sooner than later, something would have to shift.

It was no secret that my wife and I were being considered to possibly take over the Battle Creek church one day in the future, but at this point nothing was at all concrete or engraved in stone. We were just simply being considered. I remember having individuals come up to my wife and I at church encouraging us and telling us things like, "get ready because something great is about to happen," or saying things like "stay faithful because God's about to elevate you." We even had some people who would just tell us straight out that they believed Pastor Marvin was going to make us the Pastors over the Battle Creek church very soon. I believe that many began coming to that conclusion even more because Pastor Marvin was now starting to use me during their main services at the Grand Rapids Church more often. From facilitating a service, to preaching the word, people were starting to recognize that I was being used a lot more. I can honestly say that Pastor Marvin would try his best to be present for all of the services that he possibly could attend however, with so much going on, there were just some times that both Pastor Marvin and Pastor MaLinda were unable to attend. During those times, they would often ask me to fill in and preach for the services that they both were unable to make. To be entrusted with such a responsibility of stepping in for the both of them was without question an extreme honor.

The encouraging words that we were receiving from many people who believed that soon I would be shifting from being considered for the pastor position, to actually being selected as the Pastor over the Battle Creek church was absolutely humbling. But even though we knew that we were being considered, my wife and I had not received any further word that would lead us to believe that a decision like that would be unfolding anytime soon.

Word however began to spread that I was being considered for the position and even the Director of my job became aware of it. In fact, at one point my boss had a personal conversation with Pastor Marvin concerning me being considered to be the Pastor over the Battle Creek church in the future. The thought of this was starting to bring about some concerns and challenges on my job. The fact that I was already fulfilling a major role at my church was already causing a bit of conflict of its own. The underlining concern from my jobs perspective was centered around one main question, and that question was, where was my heart? Was my heart to operate fully in Para-church ministry, or was my passion more centered toward church ministry. Either one to them was absolutely fine however, to work and to balance both types of ministries effectively, they knew was an extremely difficult task for any one person to be able to handle. Ministry on just one side of those spectrums alone can become overwhelming and time consuming. The con's for trying to balance both worlds were seemingly starting to outweigh the pro's. The negative aspects ranged from the thought of one side simply not getting the full work ethic needed, to ultimately the potential burnout of the person who was trying to juggle and balance these two different ministries. Now with this new thought of me potentially being sent out as a Pastor one day in the future, not only were there questions arising as to where my heart might be, but now there were also questions arising as to where I soon might be, literally. My job had to start thinking through some very tough questions like, will he be leaving us to Pastor a church, and do we continue to invest in someone who may be soon departing us who seems to have a greater passion for church ministry, or do we use our hard earned donor based dollars and invest them into a person whose heart we are confident will fully be dedicated and devoted to Para-church ministry? A person who we know for certain will be here to build long lasting relationships with young people for the long haul. This was really starting to become an area of concern for my job, and I was really beginning to feel the tension starting to rise.

At one point it had become so intense that in order to test and evaluate where my heart was, I was placed on a probationary period with my job. Along with other requirements that was outlined for me to do during my probationary period, one of the stipulations that had been given was that I could only participate and assist in the life of the Lighthouse Grand Rapids church, but that I could not participate in the life of the Battle Creek Church location. Though I had stopped traveling down to the Battle Creek church on Mondays because of a youth program that also took place on Monday evening's for my job, to assure that there would be no conflicts (especially due to the fact that I was being considered for the pastor position), I was informed that I could not attend the Battle Creek church altogether. Beyond the conflicting dates, the thought of burnout was also a factor as well. To help assist another church in an entirely different city, along with continuing to hold my position over the high school youth ministry at the Grand Rapids church location, and then in addition to that, to also handle my fulltime job responsibilities for them, just seemed to be way too much for any one person to handle.

I agreed to my jobs stipulations and advised Pastor Marvin and Pastor MaLinda of everything that was taking place. I told them that I would not be able to assist or attend the Battle Creek church at this time, but that I was still able to participate in the life of the Grand Rapids church. Pastor Marvin and Pastor MaLinda encouraged me to stay focused and to keep pressing forward. It was a very challenging time for me, but their words of encouragement were very uplifting for my wife and I. After several weeks, the probationary period had concluded. I was assessed and evaluated based upon everything that my job had required for me to do, and I passed the requirements that they had given me. I was extremely grateful and ready to focus on the tasks ahead. I really enjoyed my job and those that I worked with. My only frustrations came from the tension that was arising due to my heart being questioned. There would be moments where the tension would get so high that I felt like quitting however, I was glad that this evaluation was able to show that I was indeed committed and dedicated to my job, and that my heart still remained with the ministry. Things started to get better, and there seemed to be a new cultivating environment that was beginning to arise. The tension and the pressure on my job was starting to subside, and things were starting to look promising again.

In my evaluation, my job had made it clear that I was able to participate only in the life of the Grand Rapids church. Though I was unable to participate or assist with the Battle Creek location, I was now put to work even more at the Grand Rapids church. Pastor Marvin and Pastor MaLinda had made a decision to start a college ministry, where they placed another gentleman and myself over it. We were responsible to manage a team of youthful leaders and to provide a service specifically geared toward college students every week. In addition to that, I was also elevated from being just the leader over their High School Youth Ministry, to now being placed in the position of being their *Minister of Education/Youth Pastor* over the entire youth ministry itself. My responsibilities had now majorly increased from only having to manage a teaching staff and class sessions for our high school students, to now having to manage and oversee all of our youth areas. My plate of responsibilities had dramatically increased.

My Sunday's where beyond exhausting. I would be with our youth during our first service, most of the time teaching or either assisting another teacher in a classroom. After the first service had concluded, it was not uncommon for someone to want to be baptized from the adult service. Because there was not a lot of people who would be available to baptize individuals, I was frequently called on to assist in this area. In between services, I would put on the garments for baptism, baptize those who needed to be baptized, and then immediately change my clothes trying to quickly prepare for our second service with our youth. After the second service would concluded, Pastor Marvin and Pastor MaLinda gave the entire third service over to the college ministry. We were now in charge of running an entire service every Sunday for our college and young adult students.

During our main services, I remember times when I would come to church relieved and excited thinking that I would finally get an opportunity to actually sit down in a service and receive a word, to only moments later be tapped on the shoulder and advised that a teacher did not show up for their assigned class. Without any question, Sunday's were beyond exhausting for me.

It wasn't too long thereafter, that my job learned of the new roles and responsibilities that I had been given at the Grand Rapids church. Though my job had made it clear during my probationary period that I could only be involved with the life of the Grand Rapids church, after becoming aware of these new responsibilities, once again the tension began to rise. With me working a full time job that provided excellent benefits and the flexibility to create my own work schedule (as I was not restricted or confined to a nine to five schedule), to them it also appeared to some degree that the church was benefiting a bit more from this work situation. As the Youth Pastor, I was providing many of the same services to my church that I was doing for my job (along with other responsibilities), with absolutely no investment from the church being yielded back in return. I was carrying out all of these tasks completely on a volunteer basis. At my church I was the Youth Pastor, I was still the head leader over our high school ministry, and I was one of the head leaders over our college ministry.

After a few months of trying to juggle all of these positions together, for a moment it actually seemed like it was all working out. I would work overtime trying hard to manage all of the areas that I had been given at my church, while at the same time trying to give my full attention and focus to my job as well. It was very demanding and extremely over taxing, but somehow by God's grace I was managing to get through it. To my job however, it was never a question of whether I could get through it or not. To them, taking on those additional responsibilities at my church was a clear indication that my heart was geared more toward doing church ministry - and with me trying to hold on to my job while working those other positions, it was absolutely unquestionably evident, that burnout for me was very soon in the horizon.

Once again, trying to prove my commitment and dedication to my job, along with not attending the Battle Creek church any longer, I resigned from each and every position that I had been given at the church. Though my wife and I were very thankful to be used at our church, and though we were also excited about the thought of being considered to possibly be sent out one day as a Pastor, the truth was that my wife and I did not really know what the future had in store for us. As far as the Battle Creek Church was concerned, we didn't know if Pastor Marvin & Pastor MaLinda was also considering other potential candidates, or if they would still even desire for us to fill such a role in the future. They could have very well made a decision to give that position over to someone else. Truthfully speaking, we were not even certain that Lighthouse Battle Creek was the place where we desired to be or more importantly, if Battle Creek was the place where God desired for us to be. While we were praying and trying to hear the voice of God for clarity and direction, it was important to me that I stayed in good standing with my job that I loved to do. But unfortunately, resigning from all of my positions and responsibilities at the church was too little too late.

I'll never forget the morning my boss informed me that we had an important lunch meeting together. He told me that our Regional Director and our Committee Chairman would be joining us for the meeting. Later that day, I was scheduled to fly out of town to Oregon for my job to do a ministry assignment. My luggage was packed and I was ready to go but first, I had to stop by this brief meeting that had been called together at the last minute. I assumed that the meeting was set up for us to talk over ways that we could better improve our area. My long plane ride ahead would give me plenty of time to think our meeting through and focus on some ideas that could help us produce whatever they were looking for. When I arrived to the restaurant and took my seat, looking around the table I could sense that something was different. As we proceeded further in conversation, it was that dry acquired uncomfortable conversation where you could tell that everyone was trying to act as if though things were normal. It felt like everyone at the table knew that something was about to take place, except for me. After ordering our food, the real reason for the meeting was revealed. It was at that moment that I was informed that I was being let go on my job. I was also informed that because their company was a non-profit ministry organization, that I was unable to collect unemployment from them while searching for a new job. In the state of Michigan, some religious or church based organizations are not required to pay unemployment to their former workers. At that time I had two young boys Eric and Zion, and my wife was now seven months pregnant with our third child. All I could think about in my mind was, *what in the world am I going to do now?* I had a house note, a family, a pregnant wife, along with many other responsibilities. How were we going to survive? I had been working at my job for the last six years and I had just received a promotion to a senior position that had given me a financial pay increase only a few months prior. Now I was being told that I was being let go after close to seven years of service, and that I could not receive one dime of unemployment while I searched for a new job.

I guess there is no easy way to let someone know that they are being terminated. I must say that those who were present at that meeting tried their best to be as courteous, gracious, and as understanding as the circumstance would allow. They even offered to extend our health insurance until my wife had our child to make sure that our expenses would be taken care of. Though this was a very kind gesture that I knew they did not have to do, my heart still melted as my future was completely uncertain.

When the meeting was over, I remember sitting in my parked car with tears in my eyes. I still had a plane to catch in a few hours as I had made a

33

decision to finish out my job right and with integrity. I remember when sharing with my wife what had just taken place, I tried extremely hard to be the strong one. I kept telling her that we were going to be fine and that God was going to come through for us. But I must be honest with you, my faith had been majorly shaken. I shed many tears on that plane ride and throughout that entire work assignment. The situation seemed so unreal yet it was very much a stark reality.

Living in moments like these can become extremely challenging because it requires us to actually have to trust God. We as believers can be so quick to pull out our *"priority faith card,"* boasting about how much faith we have when no turmoil or challenges are happening in our lives. However, it is only when the reality of devastating circumstances start to occur, that the pop quiz from our class of life begins to test what faith we actually have in us. It is also a test of our true belief and our true faith in our sovereign teacher and creator. It is in those moments that our strong voice of faith can quickly diminish into a silent whisper of immeasurable uncertainty.

It reminds me in many ways of the story of Elijah. The same Elijah that had called down fire from heaven in the presence of hundreds of Baal worshiping prophets and priest's, is the same Elijah who in the very next chapter is wandering around in a wilderness in fear of his life. This lets us know that faith must be progressive because life is continual. If we focus only on the faith that we once had in our past, we won't be prepared for the challenges that we will have to face in our future. Elijah's faith had just caused God to shift the very elements of the sky into a rain of combustible flames that did exactly what Elijah said that it would do. Yet only moments later, his faith proved to be completely shaken and depleted, and could not even withstand its ground against a simple verbal threat.

When we go through obstacles in life, many times the question is not if God can come through for us. We know that God is well able to do all things. The true question of our faith can become a fear crippling thought, will God actually come through for me? This is where our faith must graduate from being merely practical to now becoming personal. I wish I could write in this book that I simply breezed through every obstacle recorded in these pages. That I displayed nothing short of an unwavering, uncompromising, tenacity driven man of steel kind of faith. The truth however is much more humbling. I had believed God and trusted Him to move for so many others before, but I never had to personally experience faith like this for myself.

I remember sharing with Pastor Marvin and Pastor MaLinda that I had just lost my job. They had been very encouraging to me throughout the entire process surrounding my job situation. It was literally about a week after returning from my final job assignment, that I found myself sitting in the office with Pastor MaLinda, and she offered me a job to work for the church. She advised me that they were bringing me on as part-time staff for now, but that very soon they would be bringing me on as full-time staff. She told me about a grant that they were about to receive that would allow them to make me a full-time staff member. She informed me that another person and myself would have to attend weekly meetings once the grant was finalized in order for them to receive the funding. Pastor MaLinda was very supportive and she told me that both her and Pastor Marvin were very proud of us. That day she encouraged me in that office in a way that only Pastor MaLinda could do. No matter who you were, she always seemed to know the exact words to say to uplift your spirit. You could walk in her office feeling like the world was about to come to an end, but by the time you left her presence, you felt like you could conquer that same world. She let me know that God had some great and mighty plans in store for our future. She also told me that she was working on something to help additionally compensate my family and I until the grant was able to kick in, as they wanted to make sure that our family was covered and taken care of.

Not too long after that meeting, I was contacted by Pastor MaLinda and she offered me an opportunity to travel on the road with Pastor Marvin. My responsibility would be to sell his products after his events. She told me that they would pay me every time I traveled with him, and that this could help compensate our family until the grant was able to kick in. Once again God had completely blown my mind. At one moment I was at one of the lowest points of my life. I was overtaken with fear and worry, and I was being crippled by doubt. But in the very next moment, God had provided for our needs.

Many times we don't mind when God tests us with elementary circumstances and situations that we can easily breeze right through. The problem with that is, great faith is only produced through great trials. James 1:3 says, *"It is the trying of our faith that worketh patience."* The Strong's translation for the word patience is defined as, perseverance and endurance. James concludes, *"But let patience have her perfect work, that ye may be perfect and entire, wanting nothing."* Strong's translation of the word entire means to be whole and complete. In other words what James is saying is, *Faith will give you the patience to persevere and endure until God makes you whole and complete.*

Many times in the church we have a single sided view of faith. We think that faith is only used to bring us out of something. So when it seems like God isn't moving on our behalf, we easily lose sight of what little faith that we had to begin with and start giving birth to fear and doubt. What we must understand is that faith is not just used to bring us out of something, but faith's biggest and most powerful strength is to help us go through, until we are brought out. As mentioned earlier, our faith must be continually renewed and replenished, and faith is diminished when we see more of our problem than God, but faith is restored when we can see more of God than our problem. God had certainly come through for my family and I in such an incredible way. My faith had been tested, but my spirit was renewed.

As I look back now, I recognize that there have been many moments throughout this journey where it felt as if though, finally the worst was over.

It's like surviving through a massive earthquake and living in that moment of peace and tranquility after the turmoil has finally come to an end. I am told that in an earthquake, seconds can seem like minutes and minutes can seem like hours. So when the earthquake is finally over, that still moment of relief is undoubtedly overwhelming, as you thank God that you were blessed to make it out alive. The sun was shining and there was a serene calmness that seemed to now be filling and overtaking our situation. We had just survived a major earthquake. Little did we know, that deep in the billows of the ocean of life, was a shifting of our tectonic plates, and a massive tsunami was headed in our direction.

Sink Or Swim

CHAPTER THREE

STILL WATERS

One of the new responsibilities that Pastor Marvin and Pastor MaLinda had given me since I had now been hired in, was to be the Ministry Coordinator over the Battle Creek Church. Things had changed a bit since I had last visited Battle Creek. When they had first started the ministry, they started off by having Monday evening services that they would call "Hour of Power." Now it seems that the ministry had been advancing, as I was informed that they had transitioned from having one service in Battle Creek to now having two services. They would meet on Sunday evenings at 6pm, and they moved there weekday services from Monday nights to Wednesday evenings at 7pm. It was great to hear that the ministry had been progressing. One of my responsibilities as the Ministry Coordinator was to travel down and teach for their Wednesday night bible study services every week. As for Sunday services, I was told that I would be responsible to preach one Sunday a month, and that Pastor Marvin would speak for the remaining Sunday services in that month.

The Ministry Coordinator position was put into place to help us all better gage whether or not the Pastor position over the Battle Creek church would be a good fit for us or not. Would Pastor Marvin and Pastor MaLinda feel that we were able to fulfill such a demanding and critical role of ministry? On the flip side, this position also gave my wife and I some time to experience the ministry, so that we as well could decipher whether or not this was a place that we felt God was leading us to. Along with now overseeing the ministry affairs of the Battle Creek church, I was also placed back over the Youth Department at the Grand Rapids location.

Though just a few weeks ago I had lost my job which had taken some major responsibilities off of my plate, my schedule did not slow down in the slightest. Between traveling on the road with Pastor Marvin, overseeing a youth ministry, as well as now overseeing ministry affairs at a satellite church, I knew that this was going to be a very challenging season. In addition to all of these responsibilities, I would also have to figure out how to balance being a father and a husband, and somehow add all of that into the equation. It was a huge task ahead, but I was ready for the challenge.

MY FIRST EXPERIENCE BACK TO LIGHTHOUSE BATTLE CREEK

I remember the first Wednesday that I went down to teach bible study at the Battle Creek church. Because of the situations surrounding my previous job, I had not been able to attend the Battle Creek location since the initial opening services. The last time I had attended, I remembered the place being packed out with excited people ready for a supernatural encounter. I was eager to get back down there to see the progress that the ministry had made. I just knew in my mind that when I got there, the place was going to be standing room only filled with enthusiastic people ready to hear the word.

When I finally arrived, I discovered that they had changed locations from the place where they were originally having services. They were now meeting at a senior community center, and they were meeting in a room called The Country Kitchen. The room was located on the second floor of the building in a back long secluded hallway. After finally locating the room, I noticed that the tables and chairs were set up restaurant style and it had a nice open kitchen in it. I didn't know whether I should teach them the word of God, or whether I should teach them how to cook a honey glazed grilled chicken entree, served with steamed vegetables on a lightly seasoned bed of rice.

That night only six people showed up for bible study. Now let me stop here and take a moment to interject that I am not at all a person who is focused on numbers, or on how many people attend a service. I taught that night as if though the place was filled to capacity and we had an incredible time in the word. It was just a staggering shock for me to see where the ministry had now come to, compared to what I had seen before during our first visits.

On that upcoming Sunday, I went back down to the Battle Creek church, and though they were meeting in a larger size room, the majority of the seats were still empty. The attendance was definitely better on Sundays however, it was still not nearly close to the attendance that they were once receiving when the church had first opened.

I began to enquire as to what had happened, and why such a dramatic decline had taken place. If we wanted this ministry to not only survive but to grow in a healthy way, we would have to discover what was taking place that was causing people to separate or disconnect from the ministry. After enquiring, I had discovered that within that short span of time, the church had moved to three different locations. I was told that each move caused us to lose a few people at a time. Some not even by choice. I remember several individuals who months after rediscovering where we were now located, told me that they didn't even know that our church was still in town. One person said that they had come to the place where we use to have services and the ministry was gone. It was obvious that the multiple moves to different locations had an effect on the ministry.

The second thing that I had discovered was that Pastor Marvin had stopped traveling down to the Battle Creek church as often and as consistently as he did before. He would send a minister down from the Grand Rapids location who was very gifted and a very anointed woman of God. They would also use a gentleman who lived in the Kalamazoo area who was also a member of the Lighthouse church, and he would come down and speak for the Battle Creek services as well. He too was a very gifted and anointed teacher. Both of these individuals were doing very well however in all honesty, not everyone that was visiting this new church in town was coming just because of Pastor Sapp's anointing, but there were also those that were coming because of his notoriety. When some began to discover that Pastor Sapp was not coming down as frequently and as often as before, the attendance once again began to fade.

Absolutely no ministry is without its skeptics, and we certainly had our share. There were people who were awaiting the fate of the ministry. Now with the decline of Pastor Marvin's attendance, three different location changes in less than a year, and a noticeable decrease of people attending our services, some felt that it was only a matter of time before the Battle Creek Church would fold and shut down completely. And now to add misery to the equation, out of nowhere comes this new young preacher who has been appointed as the Ministry Coordinator over the entire church.

After observing the condition of the ministry, it was all too clear that this church had undergone quite a bit of challenges in its short time of existence. One of the first things that I knew the ministry needed to see was consistency. With the church seeing multiple faces coming in and out to teach and to help with the ministry, it was important for them to see a committed and a consistent presence. Every Wednesday I would take the church van up by myself and teach bible study. I would stay after the services had concluded as long as I needed to, making sure that I greeted and spoke with every person who had come out to the service. I also made it a habit to attend every Sunday service, even if I wasn't preaching that Sunday.

The second thing that I knew we needed to do was to get out of The Country Kitchen. The room was located on the second floor in a long back secluded hallway. If we wanted to see growth, we definitely needed to make sure that the atmosphere was inviting. We also needed to make sure that the ministry was in a location where it would not be difficult or confusing for people to find us. I shared these concerns with Pastor MaLinda and asked if we could possibly change our bible studies to another room that would give us more of an inviting atmosphere. I walked throughout the building and discovered a room on the first floor that was absolutely perfect. It was a nice size room as it was not too big for what we needed, yet it was not too small for us either. The room had more of a conference room type feel, and it was equipped with a ceiling projector that could easily be used to display scriptures during bible study, or the words of songs that could be projected on the screen during praise and worship. The room was also very close to two main building entrances which allowed for easy access for members, guests, and friends. After discussing this with Pastor MaLinda, she checked into the availability of the room and thankfully it was open during the times that we would need it. We officially moved our services out of The Country Kitchen into a new room that fit our needs perfectly.

Along with providing the word for bible studies, I also wanted to incorporate worship through music and song on Wednesday evenings as well. For the Sunday services, the Grand Rapids church praise team and musicians would come down to Battle Creek to lead worship however, no one from the music or worship team would travel down on Wednesdays to assist for bible study. I had a friend of mine who was an extraordinarily gifted musician and anointed singer. He was also a member of the Grand Rapids church location at the time. I asked Pastor MaLinda if it would be ok for him to come down and help us by leading worship on Wednesday evenings for bible study. She told me that if he was willing to come down and assist that it would be fine.

After receiving approval, I asked the gentlemen if he would be willing to come down and assist us in providing praise and worship for a season. He gladly agreed and made a commitment to travel down with me on Wednesdays for our bible studies. He would bring his keyboard with him and lead us in praise and worship every single week, and the presence of God would meet us in that room. On occasion his wife would also join us as well. We are to this day extremely grateful to him and his wife for traveling down to the Battle Creek Church. We also greatly appreciate the sacrifices that he made to share his anointed gifts and talents with our ministry during those times.

Through those small minor changes - being present consistently, loving on Gods people, changing our room location to a more inviting atmosphere, and incorporating praise and worship, we started to see an increase in attendance at our Wednesday night services. We went from having around six people attending to having about twenty-five people that were showing up consistently. It was a small start, but increase was starting to take place. When my wife was able to start traveling down with me after having our third child, she would join me as often as she could on the road. We started a book club where she would read through a book with the women, and I would do the same with the men. We would meet about an hour before service on Wednesdays for the book club. Doing this gave my wife and I the opportunity to spend some quality time with the guests and with the members. It also gave us an opportunity to pour into them on a more personal level as well. It was great to start seeing turn around beginning to take place in the ministry.

Though things were starting to go well with the Battle Creek church, and though we were starting to see some progress and turn around happening in the ministry, my wife and I was still in great prayer about our future concerning this church. Was this really the place where God was calling us to be in this season? The ministry had undergone some major challenges in such a short period of time. Though we were making some strides in what seemed to be the right direction, it was quite obvious that it was going to take a whole lot more tender loving care and prayer, to really get this ministry on its feet. We now also had three very young children that we needed to consider in this equation. If we took this position, we would be moving out of a city where we had family support, to a place where we hardly knew anybody at all. And now with two young children and a new born baby, was this really a move we wanted or needed to make in this season of our lives? Our heart was certainly beginning to grow attached to the people in the Battle Creek ministry, but we did not want to make such a major decision based upon how we felt. We wanted to make a final decision based upon what we felt God was leading us to do. I wanted to have an absolute assurance in my heart and spirit that this was the place where my family and I needed to be, and the answer was definitely coming up ahead.

STILL OVER YOUTH MINISTRY

At the same time that I was overseeing the Battle Creek church location, I was still over the youth ministry at the Grand Rapids church as well. The youth still met every Tuesday evening during bible study, and they also met during the Sunday services that took place at the Grand Rapids ministry. Trying to manage both the Battle Creek church and the youth ministry made for a very long and a very taxing week.

The set up that they had in operation for the youth department at that time was for the youth to meet in a more classroom style structure. Those who attended were separated by age and the atmosphere felt more like a school setting. Teachers would try their best to make their class times as interesting, interactive, and as empowering for the youth as they possibly could however, keeping the youth engaged started to become a bit of a challenge once again. Having these classrooms separated by ages also meant that for every service we had to have the proper teaching staff available to manage them. We also tried very hard to avoid teachers from experiencing burnout, as this can be a very common thing that happens in ministry. A problem that often occurs is that many times you may not have enough people who are committed to serving in the areas of ministry where there is the most need, and the faithful ones that you do have can tend to get over used. As I mentioned earlier, even with having teachers properly scheduled, it was not an uncommon thing to have a teacher who would not show up to serve during their class time. Whether it was for an excusable reason or whether it was a no call no show, the absence of a teacher would make it extremely challenging for us all.

Pastor Marvin and Pastor MaLinda were very curriculum oriented. Curriculums were presented to ensure that every teacher would be unified in what was being taught to students in the classrooms. All areas of leadership were trained under the motto of, "One Voice, One Vision." Having a curriculum provided for our teachers helped us to ensure that we were all speaking with one voice under the set vision of the church. There were times when they would allow us to teach without curriculums, but for the most part curriculums were strictly enforced.

GET A GRIP

During this time, Pastor Marvin and Pastor MaLinda presented me with a new curriculum that was called "Get a Grip." They wanted me to incorporate the curriculum into our entire youth ministry. We were able to construct a weekly youth service that we would actually call our "Get a Grip" service. The service would include our own youth praise and worship, drama, skits, games, dance, poetry, and each week the lessons would be taught from the Get a Grip Curriculum that Pastor Marvin and Pastor MaLinda had given me. We would no longer need to have teachers available for the individual classroom structure, we would just need some teachers to be present to chaperone and to also help us run the youth services.

The new format that was proposed was great however, it called for us to bring all of our classes together into one central location. The problem was that we did not have a room in our youth area located on the upper level of the Grand Rapids church, that was big enough to bring all of our young people together into one central area. We would have to use the basement of the church for our youth services, and I wanted the basement to look as youthful as possible. I went out and purchased some posters that had a gospel message on it and placed them all around the room. I also proposed to Pastor MaLinda that we purchase a small lighting system to really set a youthful atmosphere. The lighting system was approved and we were able to purchase and set it up. I had a designer friend of mine create a logo for our new Get a Grip youth service, and we made posters of the logo and hung them down from the ceiling. The basement of the church was really starting to look and feel like a youth room.

For the early morning service that would take place on Sundays, we kept the old classroom style structure of teaching, simply because there was not a lot of young people who would attend the morning services. It was at the second service that we would have more youth attend, so we started preparing to incorporate the new Get a Grip program during the second service.

The weekend of the launch of our new Get a Grip Youth Service, I was out of town with Pastor Sapp in St. Louis Missouri. I was still traveling on the road with Pastor Marvin while working hard to manage the Grand Rapids Youth Ministry and the Battle Creek Church. I remember e-mailing our Get a Grip team from my hotel room trying to make sure that we were all ready for the launch. When Pastor Marvin and I flew back to Grand Rapids that Sunday, we had to go straight from the airport to the church. When I arrived, the Get a Grip team had everything in place, and everything was set and ready to go. The youth came in and the entire service was a huge success. After flying directly in from St Louis Missouri and going straight into the launch of our new youth service, once that service had concluded, I only had a few moments to spend with my wife and kids before boarding the church van to go down to the Battle Creek church to preach for their service that evening.

I must stop here and note that the Get a Grip Team that I worked with to help run the weekly youth services were absolutely amazing and incredible people. They were extremely talented, very creative, and absolutely faithful to the call. You could see clearly that they all had a love for God as well as a love for the youth that they were serving. Their dedication and creativity birthed so many great and memorable moments that I will never forget. Not only did our Get a Grip Team impact our young people's lives, but they also greatly impacted my life as well.

With momentum starting to develop in the youth department, as well as some signs of growth starting to take place at the Battle Creek church location, Pastor MaLinda had now instructed me to once again start meeting back with our college team to try and revamp the college ministry with a hope to bring it back into full operation. So along with overseeing the Battle Creek Church, I was also leading, meeting with, and overseeing the Get a Grip youth ministry team, and I was now once again beginning to meet back with the college team trying to incorporate an on-campus ministry at various college locations, all while still traveling on the road with Pastor Marvin.

THE PASTORAL ANNOUNCEMENT

The New Year was now starting to quickly approach us. Because we generally have a lot more young people that attend our New Years' Eve Services, and because generally those type of services tend to last longer than most, I started putting together a gospel youth service called "The Remix." I was looking to bring in young local gospel artists, poets, and definitely ending off the evening with worship and the word of God. As I was speaking to Pastor MaLinda concerning the preparations for the youth Remix service, she told me that Pastor Marvin was going to be appointing new Deacons during the New Year's Eve celebration. She told me that Pastor Marvin wanted another gentleman along with myself to stand with him as he appointed the new deacons into office. She told me that we needed to go out and purchase a clergy collared shirt so that we could be properly dressed for the occasion. She said that our wives also needed to be dressed up for the occasion, as they would also be standing with us during the communion ceremony of the service as well.

On that New Year's Eve night, I remember being downstairs with the youth as we conducted the Remix service. Someone came down to advise us that it was getting close to the time for the Deacon's Ceremony to begin in the sanctuary. I quickly left the basement where the youth were meeting, and ran into the bathroom to change into my black suit and my clergy collared shirt. I rushed upstairs and stood in the hallway as we awaited to

52

enter the sanctuary with some of the other individuals that were involved with the ceremony. When we entered the sanctuary, the church was completely packed. The other gentleman that Pastor MaLinda had informed to be dressed for the occasion and myself, stood next to Pastor Marvin as we were instructed to do. I remember standing there watching as the soon to be appointed Deacons walked down the aisle. As the ceremony began, my mind was wondering back and forth to the youth service that was going on downstairs in the basement. I was thinking to myself, *I hope everything is going well. Did I tell the person who I had left in charge what was happening next?* So many thoughts were rushing through my mind at that moment. However, I begin to relax and just rest in the fact that I had an incredible team. I knew that those individuals could manage that overcrowded basement of youth, and keep everything running smoothly.

We finally came to the conclusion of the ceremony for the newly appointed deacons, and my wife and I started to head back downstairs to the youth service. When Pastor Marvin noticed that we were headed towards the door to leave, he told us to wait for a minute. When we came back to the front, he made an announcement concerning the other gentleman that was standing beside him. He said that in October he would be ordaining him as an Elder in the church. The congregation began to celebrate and applaud the announcement.

After that, came the moment that literally changed my life forever. Pastor Marvin announced to the congregation that in October of that upcoming year, I would be ordained as the Pastor over the Lighthouse Battle Creek Church. As the crowd began to celebrate, tears started to swell up in my eyes. I was really uncertain of how to respond because the moment was so unexpected. There were members from the Battle Creek church in the audience, and I remember looking out at them as they stood and applauded. I was thinking in my head, *is this really happening?* Everything seemed so unreal. I was excited, overjoyed, humbled and honored - but I was also nervous and a bit apprehensive. Yes I could oversee the Battle Creek ministry, and we did see some great successes, but did I really have what it took to be the Pastor over this congregation. At the same time, my wife and I were still praying and seeking direction as to if being the pastor over this church was even God's will for our lives, but I took this public announcement as God's confirmation.

Pastor Marvin began to share with the congregation what he and his wife had shared with us a few years back in his office. He said that when they had sons and daughters to send out in ministry, that they would make sure that none of them would ever have to go through the things that they went through when they started their ministry. He shared with us all that night a glimpse and a moment of transparency into his own personal voyage of becoming a Pastor. He said that when they had started the Lighthouse Grand Rapids church, he wished they would have had someone to set them up. He said they had to use all of their savings to start the ministry. He then shared with us that by October when he sends us out, that they were giving us a new building and that they were going to completely furnish it. He said that he was going to give us everything we needed to be effective. My wife and I just stood there in complete and total amazement. We had absolutely no clue or ideal whatsoever that any of those things were going to take place. One minute I was the Ministry Coordinator over the church, the next minute my wife and I were being announced to the congregation as the Pastor Elect and Lady Elect of the Battle Creek Church. When the announcement was over, my wife and I walked back downstairs headed to the youth service completely astonished. Everyone was congratulating us on our new elevation. We were asking ourselves, "did that really just happen?" It was such an overwhelming moment. From that earthquake of life that had hit us earlier, everything seemed to be calm. A beautiful and masterful sunset now melted into a very still ocean on the canvas of our lives. Life appeared to now be taking a turn for the better.

Sink Or Swim

CHAPTER FOUR

CLIMATE CHANGE

What an amazing season it was now starting to become. I was still the Youth Pastor at the Grand Rapids location, I had just now been appointed as the Pastor Elect over the Battle Creek Church, and I was now also starting to meet back with our college team in an effort to try and revamp and restart that ministry. Honestly, I was a bit nervous about this new ministry appointment that had just been given to me. What a great responsibility it was going to be. I was soon to be the Pastor over an entire congregation. I knew that with God's direction and help that everything would be fine, as God had never failed us yet. It was a great season of celebration as I thanked God for all of His many blessings that He had bestowed upon my family. I was extremely focused and ready to face the new level of challenges and responsibilities that this new position would bring my direction.

After a while, I started to notice that the invitations to go on the road with Pastor Marvin had begun to cease. I assumed that it was because I had so much on my plate to handle with both church ministries. The only problem was that the traveling opportunities with Pastor Marvin were being used to help financially assist my family and I until they were able to bring me on as full-time staff. It had now been several months that had passed since I had been hired in, and I was still on part-time salary. On occasion I would ask about the full-time staff position, and about the classes that I was told that I would need to attend in order for them to receive the funding necessary for my position. The common response that I would receive was that they would be getting back with me soon about it. But now that no more invitations were coming in to travel, it was starting to affect our family financially. I wasn't too worried or concerned about it, as I was confident that they would soon come through.

With me now being appointed as the Pastor Elect over the Battle Creek church, my schedule shifted. Opposed to preaching for a few selected Sunday services a month, I was now responsible for preaching at every Sunday service as well as responsible to continue teaching for all the bible studies that took place every Wednesday night. Balancing my responsibilities at the Grand Rapids church and the Battle Creek church was already a major challenge before this new appointment, but it was now starting to become even more of a challenge.

THE BUILDING

Prior to making the announcement at the New Year's Eve service that I was the Pastor Elect over the Battle Creek church, Pastor Marvin & Pastor MaLinda purchased an empty building in downtown Battle Creek. It was a blessing because with the ministry having moved three different times to three different locations, the Battle Creek church now had a place that we could finally call home. The brothers of the Battle Creek church were especially excited about this, as every week they would have to set up and breakdown equipment. Now that we had our own place of worship, they would soon be relieved of those responsibilities and would not have to worry about setting up and breaking down music and sound equipment any longer. The purchasing of this facility was also intended to send a strong message to those who may have questioned if the church was intending to leave the city or not. With the ministry now securing a building, it would show that Lighthouse Battle Creek was indeed alive and well, and that there were no intentions of the ministry shutting down or leaving the city. Word began to spread about the purchase of our new building and the excitement was starting to build at the Battle Creek church. The anticipation level was beginning to rise.

Renovations began at the new facility and everything was underway and coming along extremely well. At the rate that things were going, it was pretty clear that we would be in our new facility in no time. While the building was being renovated, I was told that someone from the city drove pass and stopped in after noticing that there were people working on the property. Unfortunately the individuals who were working on the building were not licensed contractors, and had not obtained any permits needed from the city. They were members from our Grand Rapids location who were just trying to do a few renovations on the property in an attempt to get the building ready for use. When the facility was purchased, at first glance the building did not look as if though it needed much work to be done. It was assumed that a few brothers from the church could put up some drywall, paint, add a few new light fixtures, lay some carpet and then the ministry would be in full operation. When the Grand Rapids workers told the individuals from the city that they had not obtained a permit, they were immediately stopped from moving forward with any further renovations. This began a long tedious journey with Pastor Marvin and Pastor MaLinda going back and forth to city meetings, trying desperately to gain the right to be able to use the facility that they had now already purchased.

After many deliberations and meetings with the city, they were eventually allowed to be able to use the building however, they would only be able to use it under the city's requirements and stipulations. One of which, was that the building could not be made into a church or even named or referred to as a church under any circumstances. The building that they had purchased was in a main downtown strip area that rested directly between two popular downtown bars. There were some people who thought that having a church between that kind of setting could potential bring about some challenges to those downtown businesses.

I must say that there were hardly any hurdles or obstacles that in most cases Pastor MaLinda could not deliberate her way through. She was very witty, confident, and very much quick on her feet. When you would be stuck trying your best to figure out how to solve and get through step one of a problem, in most cases, Pastor MaLinda would have long surpassed thinking through step one, and would be working well into step number eight. She knew very much how to be the sweet, loving, and very encouraging First Lady when she needed to be. But she also knew how to switch roles very quickly, and she could become the tough, aggressive, stand her ground negotiating business woman when and if the situation called for it. She was a masterful thinker, and she came up with the ideal that instead of making the facility a church, that they would make it a Business Conference Center. Doing this would allow the church to be one of its own customers, giving us the ability to rent out the Conference Center every week from ourselves. The ideal not only seemed to have resolved the issue with the city, but it also seemed to have created a potential opportunity for the church to be able to profit from this situation in the long run. Pastor MaLinda was indeed an extraordinary and a very creative woman.

Though the ideal was accepted by the city, there were however other stipulations and limitations that were put into play. Along with not being able to call the facility a church, they were also given time frames as to when the facility could actually be used for business hours. It appeared at least for now that the main hurdles that blocked them from being able to use the facility all together, had now been settled. Once those hurdles had been surpassed with the city, that's when Pastor Marvin announced at the New Year's Eve service that I was now the Pastor Elect over the Battle Creek church location. Now all that remained left to do was to renovate the property, but the renovations now also had to be done according to the city's stipulations.

At first this seemed to be a simple request, but as things begin to progress, it started to become more work than what was originally anticipated. The thought of just simply putting up some drywall, paint, and carpet, was now starting to evolve dramatically into a much more costly endeavor.

Unaware of all of this, the Battle Creek church was still very excited about the promise of having a new facility of their own. The last thing that they had heard from Pastor Marvin and Pastor MaLinda concerning the building, was that the hurdles with the city were now over and that we would soon be moving into a fully furnished facility. After a while of not hearing or seeing anything taking place, there were some from the church who began asking when the renovations were going to begin taking place at the new facility? Members were driving past the location excited and trying to see if the renovating had started yet. At this point, I unfortunately had no answers to give them. I myself did not know if Pastor Marvin or Pastor MaLinda were planning on proceeding forward with the renovations or not.

While all of this was taking place, my personal bills were now starting to add up and there was still no talk or conversations about bringing me on staff full time. Waiting for them to come through with their word and to try and help my family and I stay afloat, I started using our credit card. I had absolutely excellent credit at the time. My wife and I had never, not one time been late on our mortgage for our home, and we didn't want to start being late now. We managed the situation pretty well trying to stay financially afloat, until an escrow increase caused our house payments to go up. Once that happened, after paying our mortgage and paying our tithes to the church, we hardly had anything left over to work with for the remainder of the month. Our credit card gave us a little breathing room, but soon that card became maxed out. Once that card was maxed out, I went out and got another one. We were accumulating debt trying desperately to wait for a promise that was not coming to pass. We tried everything that we could possibly do to survive, all to no avail. We started getting extremely behind with our mortgage, and it got so bad that we were literally about to lose our home. I called to set up an emergency meeting with Pastor MaLinda concerning our situation. When we met, I shared with her what was taking place and let her know that we were in the process of losing our house. I asked her if there was anything that could possibly be done to help my family and I, and I enquired about the full-time position. I shared with her that if the full-time position was not able to come through, that I may have to get another job in order to take care of my family. Pastor MaLinda responded by sharing with us her concerns for our family. She let me know that they would not be able to bring me on full-time staff at the moment. In response to what I had shared with her about possibly having to get a job, in an effort to encourage me, she began to share with us how Pastor Marvin and herself were able to take care of their household. She told us that Pastor Marvin works three jobs in order to take care of their family. She told us that he was a Pastor, a traveling Evangelist, and a Recording Artist. She shared with us, that the only reason why she would still teach at a college, was so their family could have health insurance. She told me that she would understand clearly if I would need to obtain additional employment in order to take care of my family.

Now, I was not at all opposed to getting another job, but I was hurt and disappointed because all of this time I had been waiting on a promise that was not coming to pass. I walked out of their office that day not knowing all together what to think. I was grateful as Pastor MaLinda did give my wife and I a check that day to go toward our house, but it was not enough to stop the damage.

So I did exactly what I knew I needed to do, I went out and got a job. Through a temp-agency I got hired in at an office supply company, and I would work that job from 8am to 5pm Monday through Friday. My body was completely and totally on overload. I was still the Youth Pastor running the youth ministry at the Grand Rapids church, while still going out of town to the Battle Creek church every week to preach on Sunday and Wednesday evenings. I remember getting off of work at 5pm on Wednesday nights and having to immediately hit the road to teach at the Battle Creek church. After bible study would conclude, I would then get back on the road to drive back to Grand Rapids so that I could get up early the next morning to go to work. I had a good friend of mine who was also a Youth Pastor at a Christian Reformed Church who said to me, "do you realize that you are working the equivalent of two full-time jobs at your church." She said, "you are a Youth Pastor and the Pastor-Elect of an entire church, how are you finding the time to work another full-time job?" The truth of the matter was, it wasn't by choice. I enjoyed the office supply job that I had however, my body was giving me clear signs that this was way too much for me to handle. I was fighting to stay awoke on my job because I wasn't getting the proper amount of sleep.

I remember one day I couldn't do it anymore. I had called in to my job two times consecutively trying to catch my body up on some much needed rest. I was still on my probationary period where you were not allowed to miss a certain amount of days. I was extremely faithful to that job but my body was beginning to shut down. I just needed a day or two to be able to regroup and get some much needed rest and energy. When I came back to my job the next day, my desk had been cleared out and I was informed that they were letting me go. It was absolutely impossible for me to fulfill all of those responsibilities all at one time.

Needless to say, we lost our home. We ended up having to give up our house in a short sell. While the short sell was being finalized I had to find a place for my family and I to live. I called and talked to my father and mother who have been my strength in so many ways throughout this entire journey. I asked them if it would be ok for my family and I to come live with them for a little while until we were able to get some things worked out. With absolutely no hesitation, my parents welcomed us with open arms into their home, and allowed my family of five to stay with them. I was the Pastor-Elect of the Lighthouse Battle Creek church, the Youth Pastor over the Grand Rapids church, I was trying to restart the College Ministry, I was serving my Pastors and my church faithfully giving them all that I had, and I had just lost my house and was now moving my three kids and my wife into the basement of my parent's home.

At that moment, I had to stop and reevaluate what was most important, as well as take some time to reexamine what I needed to be involved in during this season of my life. I realized that I needed to focus my energy on operating more wisely. After praying about it, I made a decision to resign from being the Youth Pastor over the Grand Rapids Church youth department, and to also resign from trying to revamp the college ministry. If I was going to be the Pastor over the Battle Creek church soon, then I needed to focus my time and energy on where I knew I was going to be in the future. Along with the promise of a new building for the Battle Creek church, they had also talked to us about relocating our family to the city of Battle Creek. With me being elevated and becoming a Pastor of one of their churches, certainly without any questionable doubt, they would have to come through with their promise of relocating my family and I, as well as bring me on full-time staff at that time. It seemed evident and clear that I just needed to hold out for a few more months and everything would be alright. I just needed to get past this hurdle right here and my family and I would be fine. With me letting go of the other ministry responsibilities, I could now simply focus solely on the Battle Creek church. Besides, this would all be over in just a few months after our Pastoral Ordination in October.

The Battle Creek church was maintaining but certainly not without its challenges. It had now been months that had past and we still had not heard anything concerning what was taking place with the building that they had purchased. Members of the church were starting to ask more and more questions like, *are we still moving? How come they haven't started working on the building yet? What's the hold up? How long before we know something?*

I knew in my heart that if they did not come through with this building, it would be an extremely hard pill for the Battle Creek ministry to swallow. The inconsistencies of past decisions that had been made up to this point, were now starting to build up and were really beginning to affect the ministry in a negative way. Once again, we began to drop and decline in our weekly attendance during our services. I was told that there were some people who said that they would not be returning to our ministry until our church was able to become more stable. The church had been moved around to three different locations in a very short span of time, and they had now been given a promise of a new building, while months had passed without absolutely no progress being seen, or without any word be given as to whether or not they were still planning on moving forward with the building.

Before becoming the Pastor Elect, I use to meet with Pastor MaLinda weekly so that we could talk about her and Pastor Marvin's desires for the youth ministry, college ministry and for the Battle Creek church. After being appointed as the Pastor Elect, our meetings began to slow down and we would not meet nearly as frequently or as often as we had done before, especially after I had made a decision to resign from being over the youth and college ministries. In fact, the closer and closer we would get to the installation, the less and less we would meet together. There were many questions that were beginning to arise, but unfortunately at the time, we were not receiving answers.

Sink Or Swim

CHAPTER FIVE

CASTAWAY

October was now just months away which was the time that Pastor Marvin had announced that I would be installed as the Pastor over the Battle Creek Church. With October being right around the corner, I had not received any word as to what was going on or what was taking place concerning the installation. We had received many promises, but at this point, none of those promises seemed to be coming together. It had been a long road that my family and I had to endure, and my wife and I were very eager to begin preparing our family to get settled and situated in a new city. We had recently lost our home, and we were now living in the basement of my parent's house. Though my wife and I were extremely grateful to my parents for opening up their doors to us, we were looking forward to once again having a place of our own that we could call home. Traveling back and forth on the road to Battle Creek every Sunday and Wednesday alone was starting to become very tedious. It especially became a challenge when loading up our family of five and trying to take the whole family down with us. Many times we would have to leave our children in Grand Rapids with my parents, or sometimes my wife would have to stay home with the kids while I would drive up to Battle Creek to speak for the services. It was just simply too much for us to bring our entire family back and forth on the road every week. Aside from preparing and getting two young children and a baby ready and situated for an hour and ten minute drive to Battle Creek (which does not include the hour and ten minute drive back), our two oldest children were also enrolled in school in Grand Rapids. There were many nights when we would arrive home extremely late, and our children would have to get up early for school the next morning. It brought us a feeling of joy to know that this road trip both figuratively and literally would soon be coming to an end.

I was also excited that I would now be living in Battle Creek, as being in the city would allow me to be more available for the members of the church. It is challenging enough trying to Pastor a church in the same city, let alone trying to Pastor a church from out of town. With us not receiving any word concerning relocation, compensation, or even information concerning the installation, I attempted on several occasions to connect with Pastor MaLinda trying to receive clarity concerning these things. At this point, the weekly meetings that I would have with Pastor MaLinda were barely taking place any longer. With us getting so close to the month that they had set for the installation itself, I just needed to receive some clarity from them so that I could know how my family and I needed to prepare for what was ahead.

Several weeks had passed, and we still had not received any word concerning the installation or concerning our transition. When we were finally able to speak with Pastor MaLinda about this, we were told that my wife and I needed to meet with the church board concerning our transition. She told me to put together the vision of what I believed God was giving me for the Lighthouse Battle Creek church, and to be ready to present it to the board.

The Grand Rapids church had just recently purchased a new ministry campus, and my wife and I met with the board in a meeting room located at their new location. We entered into a modern yet a smaller conference room, and the meeting began. When it came time for me to present to the board, I did as Pastor MaLinda had requested. I began to share with them the vision of what I believed could take the Battle Creek church to another level. I started off by sharing with them some of the things that we had recently done to try and spark interest in the people of Battle Creek to come out and visit the church. I also shared with them some of the things that we were currently doing to try and build community in an attempt to keep those who were coming out to our services connected to the ministry. I had brought in some posters and flyers of some of the events that we were able to put together. Every event and activity that we conducted for the Battle Creek Church I would always make sure that they were cleared and approved before proceeding forward. From special services to book clubs, I expressed to them some of the things that we had used to try and build a presence within the city. I also shared with them some things that we could do in the future that I believed could build a greater presence in the Battle Creek community. The board was very inquisitive, yet very much open to hearing what I had to share. The board had many questions for me that day. In fact, I remember one of the board members sharing with my wife and I, that there are some people who may be eager to have a position like this for all of the wrong reasons. They said that a person with wrong ambitions may desire to step into a position such as this, for the benefits of being associated and connected with the status of a person who is well known. Wanting to know my heart, I was asked if I was doing this for the benefit of association, or was I doing this because I really felt led and called by God to Pastor this church. Though I could understand the context of such an inquiry, in my mind I was thinking to myself, *benefits?, what benefits?* Up to this point my family and I had sacrificed and had lost a great deal pouring into a ministry that we did not start nor even ask for. I responded back with intense passion yet I responded back respectably, as this was a very sensitive area for us. I assured the board that the reason why I was sitting at that table was certainly not based upon any benefits. I told them that the only reason why I was sitting there was because I felt led of God to move forward.

After answering the bulk of their questions, the meeting ended. The inquiry's from the board took up a good majority of our time together. Unfortunately, we did not get the opportunity to finish sharing with them the presentation that we had put together, nor did we get the opportunity to talk over the financial components of our transition.

I attempted further to try and get clarity of what was taking place, and about a week or so later, and now close to two months away from October, my wife and I was informed that the board desired to meet with us again. When we arrived to the meeting, Pastor MaLinda and only a few of the board members were present. Those that were there all began to congratulate my wife and I, advising us that they had made a decision to make me the Senior Pastor over the Lighthouse Battle Creek church. A bit puzzled, I was thinking in my mind, *I thought this was something that had already been established nine months ago.* In fact, we were now only roughly two months away from the installation itself, and these two meetings with the board were the very first and only meetings that I had ever had with them throughout this entire period of time. At this point I was a little confused however, I was just thankful that we all now seemed to be on the same page. With such a limited time remaining before October, maybe we could now prayerfully get some things finalized for my family and I. They gave us the official date for the installation and told us to give them a list of people that we desired to have invited to the ceremony as they were going to send out invitations for us. I was also told to give them my measurements for a robe that they were going to purchase for me so that I could properly be vested during the ceremony. It was a great meeting however, after it had concluded there was still no discussion, conversation, or anything mentioned concerning our family being relocated, or how our family was going to be taken care of financially. We had no idea of what the future had in store for us aside from the many promises that we had received, and so far, many of those promises were not altogether coming to pass. We needed some answers, and we definitely needed some answers right away.

SINK OR SWIM

All the invitations had now been sent out, and we were starting to get responses back from friends and family congratulating us on our new level of elevation that was soon to take place. Three weeks before the installation with still no word as to what was going to take place for my family and I, I requested an emergency meeting with both Pastor Marvin and Pastor MaLinda. That day we met in Pastor Marvin's office, and I started off the meeting by sharing with them how much we appreciated them both believing in us to send us out in ministry however, with us only being three weeks away from the installation, we wanted to find out what was taking place concerning our family. We needed to know financially what was happening, and we also needed to know information concerning the relocation of our family to Battle Creek.

This is the moment. This is the very moment when Pastor Marvin shares with his congregants and others, that there was a time when they told my family and I, "Now you must either Sink or Swim," he is referring to this very moment right here. In that meeting, they begin to express to me that at the end of December (which was two months away), that they would be cutting off all support to the Battle Creek ministry all together. This cutting away included the assistance of all ministry related support teams. They would no longer be sending their musicians or praise team down to the Battle Creek church to help assist us. Along with this, they also made a decision to cut off absolutely all funding and all financial support to the Battle Creek church. This even included the cutting away of the part-time salary that I was currently receiving from them. Along with this, there were no plans in place for relocating my family and I to Battle Creek. And to make matters even worse, they had made a decision to cut off the transportation that they were providing for us to get back and forth to the Battle Creek church. Prior to this decision being made, they would provide their church van for us to be able to use on Sundays and Wednesdays to get back and forth to the Battle Creek services. This was done mainly to provide transportation for their ministry teams that would come down to serve with us on Sundays however, on Wednesdays, though none of their ministry teams would come down to assist us, they would still allow me to use the church van because my truck was not at all in the best condition to get back and forth on the highway. But now that their ministry teams would no

74

longer be coming down to assist us on Sundays, there was no need for them to provide transportation at all. It would now be my responsibility to figure out a way to get back and forth to the Battle Creek church on my own at least twice a week. You also remember that fully furnished building that they were going to give us, not any more. They had made a decision not to finish the building because the cost of remodeling the facility according to the city's stipulations, far exceeded what they were willing to pay.

While I sat on that coach in Pastor Marvin's office hearing those words, my mind went back to the day that I was standing in front of the church several months prior. It went back to the day that he had announced that I was going to be the Pastor over the Battle Creek church. Almost like a movie scene, there was a moment that kept replaying over and over again in my mind. The scene was not of Pastor Marvin sharing with my wife and I all of the many promises and great things that they were going to give us. But rather, it was of the moment where he shared with us the promise that he and Pastor MaLinda had made to each other. He looked me directly in my eyes that night while sharing with my wife and I, that they had made a promise to themselves that when they had sons and daughters in ministry, that they would make sure that none of them would ever have to go through what they went through to start their ministry.

I sat on that couch in disbelief. We were literally three weeks away from the installation and invitations had already been sent out. Many of our family, friends and the Battle Creek church members were excited about what was set to take place. With all of the excitement in the air, I had just received word behind the scenes that all support to the ministry was about to soon be completely cut off. Surprisingly enough, out of all of the things that were said and presented to us in their office that day, what hurt me the most was the fact that they were not the ones who had even called for that emergency meeting... I was. Had I not contacted them requesting that meeting three weeks prior to the installation, I'm not sure when we would have been informed that all support was soon to be severed.

My wife and I left that meeting stunned and in sheer amazement of what had just taken place. It was a quite drive back to my parent's house where we were living. Once again I tried hard to fight back the tears from falling while being in front of my wife however, several tears somehow managed to slip pass my line of defense, somehow making its way down the side of my cheek. What were we going to do now? The church was still very small and barely able to financially take care of itself let alone a family of five. At that time, the churches attendance was not very large at all. When we would have a decent size crowd, we would have roughly thirty people in attendance. That was considered a good Sunday service for us. But even with that size of a crowd, a good portion of those who would attend would often be visitors from other churches. We unfortunately had already begun to decline in attendance, as we were still trying desperately to recover from some of the previous inconsistencies that the ministry had gone through in the past. Now with this fresh and harrowing sting of their final promise to provide the Battle Creek church with a building completely falling through, and with Pastor Marvin now completely turning the ministry over to a very young man that people were still learning and getting to know, and with the presence of the Grand Rapids ministry teams soon to be completely removed including the presence of music, and with the transportation being cut off and me now having to find a way to get back and forth to Battle Creek weekly for services, and with all financial support to a ministry that was already losing life fast about to be completely cut and removed, the future for this Battle Creek church was looking rather dark and bleak. We were undoubtedly without any question placed into a Sink or Swim situation, and it would take an absolute miracle from God if this ministry was going to somehow survive.

Once I got back home to my parent's house, I locked myself in their basement and stayed down there for hours just praying and crying. I thought in my mind, *God what's going on? What do I do?* I felt such a heavy weight and a heavy burden resting on me. I felt extremely pressured into this moment. I remember at one point, all I could do was just weep before God. It was one of those cries where I couldn't say anything. I had to let my heart and soul speak for me because my mouth was at a loss for words.

The very next day, I sent Pastor Marvin and Pastor MaLinda an e-mail, and in it I tried to be as respectful as I possibly could. Even in the hardest and most challenging times, I have always tried to show great respect and honor toward them both. I thanked them for meeting with us, and I advised them that our meeting together had sparked a lot of questions. In that e-mail, I listed a few of my concerns and shared some of the more hard pressing questions that were on my mind at the moment. Truth be told, I had a whole lot more questions than what I had placed in that e-mail. I was a young man with a young family that knew absolutely nothing about starting a church, or even how to successfully run the business side of a church. The devastating blow was that none of those things were ever taught to us or even discussed with us before this moment. We had close to a year since the first official announcement had been made that I was going to become the Pastor over the Battle Creek Church. There was ample time for us to have received proper training and some understanding as to how to run a ministry. We could have even properly prepared for such a separation in advance, making the cutting away of any and all ministry support and finances a much easier transition. But unfortunately, none of these things were ever discussed with us. As I mentioned before, I had stepped into a Pastoral role some years back helping a friend of mine out with his church, but even back then, I had absolutely no clue or knowledge as to how to run a church administratively. I just enjoyed preaching and teaching God's word and helping people to change their lives for the better. But now because of my lack of understanding, and due to this very short amount of time that remained, it left me trying desperately to enquire as much information as I possibly could all in that one e-mail.

Pastor MaLinda responded back in an attempt to try and give me some answers to my questions. Her e-mail response actually generated for me a series of more and more questions. It was all too clear that the answers that I needed could not be given merely through back and forth e-mail correspondences. In her response, Pastor MaLinda shared with me that the board would be meeting together on that next day at the church. She told me that if I desired, I could come and address any further questions and concerns that I may have with the board at that time. I responded back to Pastor MaLinda confirming our attendance, and I also requested that she would be present with us at the meeting as well.

On that next day, my wife and I attended the board meeting. We met in a back room adjacent to Pastor MaLinda's office were we all sat around a board room table. After the meeting was opened up with a word of prayer, I was then given an opportunity to share and express my heart. I began to explain to the board that I strongly felt that the separation that was taking place between the Lighthouse Grand Rapids Church and the Lighthouse Battle Creek Church was not being done in a healthy or in a proper way. I shared with them, that just a few days earlier I had a meeting with Pastor Marvin and Pastor MaLinda, and my wife and I was informed that all support, including financial support for the Battle Creek Church and for my family was being cut off completely. With less than a month away from the installation, with invitations already sent out and with a ministry in Battle Creek that was now excited for this transition, we were just now being informed of such a major and detrimental decision literally only a few weeks away from the installation itself. I explained to them that I understood clearly that the Lighthouse Battle Creek Church could not be supported by the Grand Rapids Church forever. I was not at all disputing the need for a separation, I was only disputing the timing that they were giving us for our separation. I advised them that I was coming to the meeting to see if they would at all be willing to consider giving us a small extension of support to assure a healthy transition.

Not too long back, my wife and I had given birth to our youngest son Jathen. I shared with the board a story of something that had taken place in the delivery room with my youngest son. At that time, we already had two handsome young boys which were both delivered through a cesarean delivery. During my wife's last pregnancy, because we knew that she was going to have another cesarean delivery, we both agreed on a decision for her to get her tubes tide during the cesarean surgery. So on the day of my youngest son's delivery into this world, one of the nurses on duty was aware that my wife was having her tubes tide. Through our conversations, she also discovered that I had never cut the umbilical cord for any of our other sons. From that moment on, in a nice yet in a very insisting manner, the nurse continually encouraged me to cut the cord for what could possibly be our final child. Already a bit skirmish from just merely being in the delivery room itself, I politely and continually rejected her offers. After much persistence and realizing that this nurse simply was not going to take no for an answer, I finally agreed to cut the umbilical cord for my son. When it was time to cut the cord, the nurse called me over and handed me what appeared to be a pair of medical scissors. A bit anxious and excited as I was laying eyes on my son for the very first time, the nurse had turned away for just a brief moment and I started to go toward the chord to cut it. When the nurse turned around and saw that I was about to cut the cord she said, "NO STOP!!" A bit shaken from her tone and expression, she had my undivided attention. She began to explain to me that when you cut the umbilical cord, you cannot cut the cord anywhere you desire, but you must cut the cord in the right place. She told me that if you cut the cord too close to the baby, you could potentially do harm to the baby. She then showed me the proper place where I needed to cut the cord to separate my son from his mother. After sharing that story with the board, I informed them again that I knew a separation needed to take place for the Battle Creek ministry, but that it was very important for us to cut our connections in a proper and a healthy way. I told them that cutting their support too soon could potentially do more damage to us than good. I requested an extension of at least an additional two or three months of help and support so that we could properly be released. With the final two months we had left, adding this extension would give us roughly four to five months altogether to effectively prepare for a proper separation.

After I had finished sharing my heart, Pastor MaLinda responded by telling my wife and I that it was their intent to inform us much sooner about them cutting off the financial support to the ministry. She informed us that there was a person on the board who they had assigned to share that information with us, but for some reason the information was never passed on. She began sharing with my wife and I how starting the Grand Rapids church years ago was a major faith walk for both Pastor Marvin and herself. She began to encourage us to have faith and to believe God. Others from the board also began to join in, encouraging us also to believe God and to step out on faith. I expressed to them some of my other concerns and apprehensions, and my heart was beginning to sink deep into my chest, as it was starting to become clearly evident, that receiving an extension to help the Battle Creek ministry or to even help my family, was not about to happen. Pastor MaLinda shared in that meeting that she felt that I had a clear idea of how I wanted to run the ministry. She advised my wife and I that they had made a decision not to make me a Campus Pastor, but that they had made a decision to make me the Senior Pastor over the Battle Creek Church. She said that the difference between the two is that with a Campus Pastor, the decisions are made solely by the Senior Pastor of the main campus church, and that the satellite church is then supported in every way by the main campus church itself. But with me now being installed as the Senior Pastor, they were giving me the liberty to run the ministry and make my own decisions for the church however I desired. She advised us that with this understanding, it is the responsibility of that church to then support itself financially.

The meeting concluded and no extension was granted. Since the invitations for the ordination had already been sent out, and with everyone including the Battle Creek members excited about this ordination (having absolutely no clue of what was taking place), I was left in my mind with a very daunting and challenging decision. I really felt pressured into this moment, and it was looking absolutely nothing like what had been spoken to us much earlier. We had once been told that they were going to provide us with everything that we needed to be effective, to now being told, that we now must either Sink or Swim. These were two extremely and totally different dynamics.

I did not have a lot of time before the installation itself but in my mind I had to make a decision. Do I continue to proceed further and follow Pastor MaLinda and the boards advise to "step out on faith" in this Sink or Swim situation, or do I walk away from everything now? We had built some great relationships with many people at the Battle Creek church. As I thought through this process, I kept seeing their smiles and hearing their testimonies in the back of my head. Some thanking us for pouring into their lives, others thanking us for coming to their city. There were a few people who had even told us that they felt like God had specifically sent us to Battle Creek just for them and their family. But were we only sent to that city for a small season, as there are some assignments that God will give you that are not always permanent assignments. Was that God's intent for us in this situation? Do we walk away from everything now?

I prayed and asked God for clear direction. Honestly, walking away from this church in the natural sounded and looked a whole lot better than holding on to this withering ministry. As I prayed about what I should do, God began to bring back to my remembrance the situation that I had went through many years prior with my friends church. I remembered when I agreed to help out his ministry, they too were going through some very difficult and challenging hardships at the time. God reminded me that one of my very first gifts after accepting that assignment was an eviction notice that was greeting me at the front door of their church. The church was homeless, yet God still provided. The church had no money to offer me for compensation. In fact, it was evident from just the eviction notice alone, that the church was struggling to take care of itself. Yet again, somehow and in some way, God would always seem to make sure that my family's needs were always met. What I did not realize then, was that sometimes God will allow you to go through things in your past, to prepare and to train you up for something greater in your future.

Never ever despise the painful circumstances that you are facing right now. There is always a lesson in everything that you go through. What you may be trying to avoid today, may be the very key ingredient that unlocks what is needed to give you what's necessary to be successful in your future. You may cry about it now, you may even get frustrated while going through the process, but if you endure to the very end, you will thank God later, that He trusted you with trouble. It is because trouble is one of the major ingredients necessary to producing triumph. If you don't go through something, you will never have the amazing assurance that God is able to bring you out. In fact, to be delivered from something literally means to be set free or brought out. So if you don't go through it, you will never experience God's true deliverance power.

Some people may even ask why would God allow you to face such devastating obstacles. You must understand that God is able to see clearly the entire portrait of our lives. The scriptures give us the understanding that God is omnipresent. Webster defines omnipresent as meaning: [being] present in all *places* at all times. Webster did an incredible job of defining the word omnipresent however, with God it goes a step further. God is not limited to only being in every "place" at the same time, but God also defies the very nature and the very element of "time" itself. This means that just as God is living in our present day now, He is already very much alive and living in our future. Because of this, many times when He allows us to go through various situations in life, He is able to custom design our circumstances not based upon where we are right now, but based upon where He is in our future. We also know that every challenging obstacle that comes our way is not always sent from God. There is an old saying that we would often hear in church, and it says, "What the devil meant for bad, God will turn around for my good." Yes even the enemy will send some things your way, especially when he knows that you are chosen by God. Most often his attacks will have one primary focus at hand, and that's to steal, kill, and to destroy. But with God's guidance, He can take the very things that the enemy sent to kill you, and use them as fuel to propel you into your promise. And finally, when everything is all said and done, and you've past the test, and you've arrived to your place of destiny, the stage will be set where the only person who can get the glory for you surviving through every painful pitfall, every obstacle, and every stumbling road block in your life, is God Himself. You nor anyone else, will be able to take the credit or the glory for your triumphant victory..... only God.

In my final thoughts and prayers concerning whether I should proceed further with the ministry, I had learned some time ago, that deep in the middle of the ocean when a ship is sinking, it is customary that if there is even so much of a glimpse of hope that the ship may be able to possibly survive, the Captain of the ship is to remain on board until every possible option has failed, and until every person has safely departed from off of the ship. The more and more I prayed about the situation, the more and more I kept feeling as if though abandoning this church was not an option.

I kept rehearsing that last and final meeting with the board over and over in my mind. I came to the conclusion that since there were two months before all support would be cut off completely, that I would have to work those two months extremely hard giving it absolutely everything that I had. My hope was that after Pastor Marvin, Pastor MaLinda, and the Grand Rapids Board would see some progress in the ministry from those last two months, that maybe... just maybe before our support would be completely terminated, we could revisit the situation and prayerfully a more reasonable and suitable plan for a successful departure could be set into motion. I also remembered from my previous non-profit job that in the state of Michigan, religious organizations were not required or obligated to pay out unemployment. So I really had to work extremely hard to make sure that these last two month's counted. That night I e-mailed Pastor Marvin, Pastor MaLinda, and the entire Grand Rapids church board and advised them that I did need to have more faith, and I assured them that I was ready to take on the challenge ahead.

THE INSTALLATION

As I'm sure you can imagine, the last couple of weeks flew by extremely fast. The members of the Battle Creek church were excited, all the while they were still oblivious as to the circumstances that surrounded their Pastor and First Family. The ordination was set to take place at the Grand Rapids church location, so several members and friends from the Battle Creek church drove up to Grand Rapids to be a part of the installation ceremony. I remember arriving to the church that day. It was all starting to become a reality. I was now just moments away from being installed as the Senior Pastor over the Battle Creek Church. I was taken to a back room were my mom and dad joined me. I remember them both hugging me, and them both telling me how proud they were of me. My father looked me in my eyes and said, "you're going to do great son." Moments later, someone came in to escort my parents into the gymnasium where the service was going to be taking place. My wife was in the restroom getting ready, and I vividly remember being in that back room by myself just starring outside of a window. It was one of those chilly Michigan days, but it was a beautiful one. As I looked out the window, the sun was beaming through the trees in which many were displaying their stunning and radiant Fall colors. It was complete silence in that room. It's hard to articulate what I was feeling at that moment. I knew that in the next few minutes, my life was about to change dramatically. In spite of the since of an uncertain future, there was an unusual calmness and peace that had come over me. I stood there, starring out of that window feeling the serene peace of God's presence surrounding me.

A person came in the room to get me, and I was then escorted into a hallway were both Dr. Marvin and Dr. MaLinda were awaiting. My wife also joined us there as well. I remember being told to stand next to Pastor Marvin as we stood awaiting to walk toward the gymnasium. When we finally arrived into the gym, there was a nice crowd of family and friends who had come out to support. All of the Battle Creek members that had traveled down were asked to sit up front as later in the program they would participate in the ceremony as well. Two chairs were placed in the very front of the church where my wife and I were seated. Pastor Marvin began sharing with us what he had called, "A Father, Son, Daughter Chat." To be quite honest with you, as encouraging as the message may have been, while

Pastor Marvin was speaking, my mind was going in and out of his message. I was thinking about the task that lied ahead of us. I was thinking about my beautiful wife who was sitting beside me. I was also thinking about our three children who were seated next to their grandparents. I thought about the Lighthouse Battle Creek members sitting behind me, who were placing their confidence in the leadership of a young man who was unsure of what was in store for our ministry. That thought alone was very humbling yet a very weighty thought in and of itself. Though all of this was being placed on my shoulders right here in this moment, throughout the entire ceremony I had an assurance in my spirit that everything was going to be okay. I was also still hopeful that if we could just somehow show some progress in the final two months, that we could hopefully come back to the table to discuss a possible extension of support, especially for my family and I.

When we got to the end of the ceremony and Pastor Marvin was about to dismiss the service, he turned and asked us, if we wanted to say something. I paused for a moment. I did share that day, and though we were not at all set up in the best conditions, we still loved Pastor Marvin and Pastor MaLinda both very dearly. I celebrated Pastor Marvin, sharing with them how extremely grateful I was and I thanked them for believing in me. A told them a story of a time my father and I went to a service when I was a young boy and Pastor Marvin was present at that service singing. I did not know then that I was looking down from that balcony at a man that would later become my future Pastor. After thanking him, and after thanking all of those who had come out to support, the ceremony concluded, and now everything was official.

I am sharing the following information here ONLY because there have been some individuals who have greatly been misled. There are some people who were given the impression that we were released and sent out with a whole lot of money. I have had some individuals share with me that they were told that the Battle Creek church received $50,000.00 when we were released to start the ministry off. There are others who had the impression that we had received even more than that to get the ministry off of the ground. Where those figures came from, that I am uncertain. What I do know, is that none of those figures are even remotely close to being true or accurate. The only financial gift that the Battle Creek church received from the Grand Rapids church for our launch, was for them to continue to take care of the final two months of our ministry expenses. No other financial gift was given to us from the Grand Rapids church at all. At the installation service itself, two offerings were taking up from our guests, friends, family, and even the Battle Creek members themselves to help support the launch. The first offering that was taken up was specifically for the Battle Creek Church itself, and the second offering that was taken up was specifically for my wife and I. In the second offering, Pastor Marvin and Pastor MaLinda publically gave my wife and I a gracious seed of $2,500.00, in which we were very grateful. The rest of both of the offerings that were taken up were not much at all. Later we did receive a final check that was given to us from the Battle Creek savings account which included the last few Battle Creek offerings. From all of this it gave us a small cushion to work with, but it was not nearly enough to keep both the ministry afloat and take care of my family. One area would surely have to go without if we were going to survive.

Sink Or Swim

CHAPTER SIX

DEEP IN THE OCEAN

Now being the Senior Pastor over the Lighthouse Battle Creek Church, with only two months before all of our support was going to be completely cut off, I knew I needed to work hard and I knew I needed to work fast. My first goal was to try and find us a new place of worship, as the facility that we were currently renting from had undergone new management. Along with this new management also came new rental prices, and their costs increased. I knew that we would have to find another location, and I knew that we would need to find one relatively soon. I was open to any options that we could possibly find, even if it meant that we would have to rent or lease at a different location again until we could find something more permanent. My goal was to try and find an owner who would be willing to possibly do a lease with an option to buy agreement with our church. It was also important for us to find a location where we knew that we could be planted for a while. With all of the moving around that our church had previously undergone in the past, and especially after the unfortunate final disappointment of not receiving the furnished building that the Battle Creek church had been promised, I knew that we definitely needed to establish some stability in the city.

The moment I was informed that they would no longer be providing us with the building that they had promised, I immediately started looking for a different location even prior to the installation taking place. When my wife and I would come in town for services, we would drive all around the city of Battle Creek, search real estate websites, we would even ask around town trying to enquire if anyone knew of any buildings that were for sale or lease. In our quest to find a new location, we discovered a nice yet a very small church facility that was for sale. It was a tiny building that could seat approximately 50 people comfortably. Though it was small in size, it was the perfect fit for our church. The facility had two small classrooms in the very front of the building, along with one small office space that was located right next to the sanctuary. It was quaint, but it was a place where our ministry could grow.

The name of the church that was selling the property also happen to be named Lighthouse, so as we walked throughout the small building, there were posters around the facility that said Lighthouse on them. My wife and I took that as a possible sign that this could actually be our new place of worship. We were so excited about this discovery that we set up another time to walk through the building, and this time we invited our church to come and check out the location with us. We were only suppose to be walking through the facility to view it, but since the building was so small, we were done looking at the entire property in about two minutes - literally. Once we had finished our walk through of the church, we all gathered inside of the sanctuary and we all began to praise God. A few of our church members made their way up front to the stage area and formed a small little choir. The church had an old organ in the sanctuary. It was far from a Hammond B3, but it provided us with enough sound for us to get our praise on that day. Our small newly formed choir started singing an oldie but a great gospel classic. They sang Kirk Franklin's song, "He's Able." You could feel the presence of God moving in that room. We praised God so much in that small little building, that when we looked in the back of the sanctuary, the realtor who was an older Caucasian gentleman, and a very nice yet a reserved man, had tears in his eyes. After we were finished viewing the property, still a bit moved by what he felt in that sanctuary, the realtor came up to me and told me that he was going to do everything he possibly could, to try and help us get into that building.

With the facility being so incredibly small, the asking price was extremely affordable. Because of how low the price was and due to our desperation to find a new place for our ministry, I was open to trying every possible option that was out there for us to secure this building, including attempting to try and get a bank loan. I figured that if we gave it a shot, the worst thing that the bank could say was no. I knew that if we were somehow able to get approved for a loan, that our payments for a loan of that size would not be that much monthly and our utility costs would also be low as well. Securing this facility would not only set us up to pay a much lower amount than what we would have to pay renting at our current location, but it would also allow us to have a place of our own that we could finally call home. This was looking like an incredible opportunity. The realtor was optimistic and believed that he could help us get the bank loan that we needed however, with us having very little financial records, and with us having absolutely no assets or collateral of any sort to our name, our chances of receiving a bank loan (even for such a small amount) was very slim. It did not help that around this time the economical state of our country was on a massive decline. Due to the conditions of our economy, banks were clamping down immensely on giving out loans to businesses, corporations, and even ministries that were far more established then what we were. Securing a bank loan with these type of conditions surrounding us would prove to be nearly impossible. A lease with an option to buy agreement was also out of the question. The realtor informed me that unfortunately the previous church that occupied the building still owed on the property. He told me that because of how low the asking price already was, and because they still owed the bank that they would not be able to negotiate or to even consider any other purchase options other than an outright sale. The realtor did keep his word trying his best to get us into that building, but it was obvious that it was going to take much more than what we had initially anticipated.

Working extensively hard to try and discover a way to secure a facility, with what seemed like such a small amount of time, our two months of support from the main church campus would come to an end. The ministry teams that were coming down to support the Battle Creek church from the Grand Rapids location would no longer be coming down to assist us any longer. As far as the attendance was concerned, nothing too much had changed. And with the Grand Rapids teams no longer coming down to assist us, there would be even less people in attendance, as their presence made our service's seem a bit fuller.

One of the most challenging transitions was when I received a call from the Grand Rapids church office for me to turn in the key to the church van. We would no longer be able to use their vehicle for transportation to get back and forth to the Battle Creek church. There were no inquiry's of any kind made whatsoever to check and make sure that my wife and I had safe transportation to be able to get back and forth to the Battle Creek church on our own. I had simply received a telephone call to turn in the church van key to the office as soon as I possibly could. No final board meeting or last evaluation with the Grand Rapids Church took place to assure that we were all set for this transition. Ready or not, this ministry was now fully in my hands. All financial support to the ministry was completely cut off, and the church was still far from being in a financial position to be able to support itself and to support my family. As I mentioned earlier, one of the two areas would have to go without in order for the other one to have any potential hope of survival. For the time being, my wife, my three boys, along with myself would have to continue to live in my parent's home in Grand Rapids until things would be able to change.

Some of the band members as well as a few of the singers that were coming down from the Grand Rapids music team, shared with my wife and I that they had been informed that their assignment at the Battle Creek church was over. After being told that they no longer had to come down to support the church any longer, they shared with us that there was no way that they could leave our ministry like that. Those individuals made a decision to continue to travel down to the Battle Creek church every single Sunday to help us with our services. They told us that they would continue to help and support our ministry until we were truly able to function and stand on our own. And they all absolutely kept their word. Their commitment and their passionate heart toward our ministry blessed us more than they will ever know. With there no longer being a van provided for transportation, these individuals would cram up into cars to drive down every week to make sure that our services were fully covered. After they would finish singing and even playing instruments for praise and worship, they didn't start packing up their instruments in the middle of service to leave early like I've seen some musicians do. They would travel down to Battle Creek, make it in enough time to set up their instruments before the service started, they would then give all that they had to usher us into the presence of God through song, and then they would not leave until our service had concluded, knowing that they had a long drive back to Grand Rapids ahead of them. There were many times that the only way that we could pay them was with some gas money and a bite to eat from a nearby fast food restaurant, yet not one time did anyone of them ever complain. I cannot even begin to articulate or put into words our gratitude toward those individuals who stretched beyond their obligations, and continued to help support our ministry in one of our greatest times of need.

To see a group of people get out of a crammed up vehicle (after an already long day) from an hour and ten minute road trip ready to serve God's people, then to give their absolute all during the service and cram back into a car for another hour and ten minute road trip back home, is something that the Lighthouse Battle Creek Church family and I will never ever forget. We are extremely grateful for everyone of those individuals, and we appreciate their sacrifice, kindness, service, love and their support. There are memories that were created during those moments that will NEVER be forgotten (*like the Arby's Cheesecake bites - smile*).

The Battle Creek church had made some progress in those last couple of months, but not much. I worked over time trying hard to build a stronger sense of family and community in our congregation. Though our support had now been cut off, I still had hopes that somehow we could rebuild this ministry.

While we were yet optimistic concerning the small church building that we believed could soon possibly become our new facility, there was a lady who lived in Battle Creek that would visit our services quite frequently. Though we did not know who she was, we would see her often in the audience. One evening after a bible study, the young woman approached me and asked me if I felt like the small church building that we were pursing was the building that God desired for us to have? I told her that we were still praying about the facility but that we were open to whatever God's will and desire may be for our ministry. She then told me about another facility that was for sale not too far away from the small building that we were currently pursuing. She encouraged my wife and I to take a moment to drive past the building before heading back to Grand Rapids that night. She told me that after we had an opportunity to take a look at the property to pray about it, and let her know if we felt like God was saying anything to us concerning the building. After I agreed to drive past and check out the facility, she gave me the address and we departed ways.

That night my wife and I drove up to the place that the lady had directed us to. When we pulled into the parking lot, our first initial reaction was that we must have mistakenly come to the wrong place. The building that the lady had directed us to was a former elementary school that was now vacant and for sale. What the lady did not know, was that months prior to this moment, my wife and I were driving around the city of Battle Creek and found ourselves sitting in that same exact parking lot, dreaming of the many possible things we could do with a building like that. That same night some months ago when we had first discovered the building, my wife and I told God that if He ever blessed us with a building like that, we would use it for His glory. Though we knew back then that for us to even attempt to purchase a building of that magnitude would be nearly impossible for us to do, we were so drawn to the facility that night, that we still wrote down the realtor company's name and looked up the buildings information online. When we found the property online and discovered what the asking price was for the building, my wife and I jokingly said to ourselves, "I guess that place won't be Lighthouse," and we continued to move on with our search. We had not seen nor had we passed the building again since that moment. Yet here we were once again, sitting in the same exact parking lot of a vacant elementary school that we had once found ourselves dreaming in.

When I spoke again with the young lady who had sent us to check out the building, she asked me what my wife and I thought about it. I told her that we thought the place was absolutely amazing. I also told her about our first encounter with the building. I shared with her how a couple of months back my wife and I sat in that same parking lot dreaming of the many possibilities that could be done with that building. She smiled at me and said, "maybe God is up to something."

My mind started to race with visionary thoughts as I began to imagine the endless possibilities. We would literally have an entire school that we could transform into a ministry campus. As I began to visualize what the inside of the building looked like, and as I began to travel down each hallway in my mind, I envisioned what each classroom could be used for. It was then that reality abruptly interrupted my ambitious thoughts.

For one, I knew for certain that we would not be able to get a loan for the amount that the building was originally listed for. And even if somehow we were able to slip through the cracks and get approved for a loan, with a ministry of our size, would we be able to keep up with the monthly mortgage payments, maintain the facility, or even pay the monthly utilities cost? I have seen many ministry's completely fold, all because they made an ambitious decision to purchase something that seemed like a blessing at the moment, but later turned out to be a dreadful curse in disguise.

The next time I spoke with the lady that directed us to check out the building, I shared with her my concerns and reservations of pursing after it. What I did not know, was that the lady worked for the school system, and she wanted to see if she could gather some information on the building for us. She encouraged me to wait before making any final decisions. She told me that she would speak with a few people to see if she could get a hold of some of the utility reports for us to be able to review. She told me that after I reviewed those reports to really go before God and pray about this, and to then let her know what our final decision would be. The lady came through with her word and provided me with the utility reports as she had promised. The utility costs were certainly on the higher end, but surprisingly they were not nearly at the level that I had expected them to be. If we were to somehow get this building, it would definitely be a MAJOR stretch for us and a complete and total walk of faith.

My wife and I did as the lady had suggested and prayed hard about whether we should pursue after the building or not. As I prayed about it, I must be honest with you, I still had many apprehensions in my mind. It was great to discover that the utility costs were not as astronomical as I had originally expected however, the real question was, could we even get a loan to purchase this building. And if we did get the loan, how much would a monthly payment for a mortgage on an entire school cost? Though my mind could not altogether process everything, as we were praying about it, oddly enough I kept feeling in my spirit as if though we needed to proceed further.

We finally made a decision to move forward with caution. We would continue to prayerfully progress forward however, if at anytime we felt as if though the situation at hand would harm the ministry, we would pull back before making a final permanent long-term decision. We spoke with the young lady and shared with her that we were willing to move forward. She was very much an encouragement to my wife and I, and she expressed to us how she believed God was going to make a way for us to have that building. She encouraged my wife and I to trust God. She then told me that she was going to set up a meeting for us to sit down directly with the Head Director in charge over that school building. She told me to put together a proposal, and in that document to include an amount of what our ministry would be willing to offer the district for their school. In a loving yet a firm way, she told me not to be afraid to put down whatever amount I felt like God was placing in my heart to write. Once again she encouraged me to trust God, and to believe whatever I felt God was leading me to do.

Honestly, we hardly had any money to our name and nothing at all substantial to offer the district. I wrestled in my mind with a few possible figures, and by faith and with the leading of the spirit, I put together a proposal to present to the district. The amount that I had proposed to them was a lot of money for us, but I knew that it would be an extremely low offer to the district for the school.

The meeting was set with the Director and the day came for us to meet with him. The only other individual who attended the meeting with my wife and I that day, was the young woman who had been working with us and had set up the meeting. In the parking lot before we entered the building, we huddled together and said a very simple prayer, "God today let your will be done." As we started to walk into the facility, immediately all of the reasons why the school district should say no to us started over-clouding my mind. In addition to the meager offer amount that we were presenting them, I was a very young preacher who they knew absolutely nothing about. I had no history with them at all and I was a new face to the city. We had no mutual outside acquaintances where they could check my track record to see if I was really able to come through with what I said. And honestly, our name unfortunately had a negative stain on it with the city because of the building that had been purchased by the Grand Rapids church in downtown Battle Creek. It had now been a couple of years and the building remained vacant and unused. Though the Grand Rapids church owned the building, many people would still associate the building with the Battle Creek Church. We were continually asked about the facility, with many in the city wondering if anything was ever going to be done with the property. Unfortunately, the decisions that were made back then were still affecting us in a negative way now though we were trying desperately to move forward.

I was also told that many other well established businesses and organizations had attempted to purchase the school property at one time, as this building was one of the districts premier schools in Battle Creek. In spite of other peoples many attempts and efforts to purchase the building, for some reason, all of the previous attempts would fall through. I started thinking to myself, if well established businesses with money could not get the building, what kind of chance do we have being a ministry with hardly any money?

Sometimes God will place you in situations where all you have is Him. You may not have the resume, you may not have the credentials, you may not have the support that you need. You may not have the influence that others may have, and you may not even have a dime to your name, but if you have God, you have everything that you will ever need. In that short walk in the hallway that led to the Director's office, I felt God reassuring me that He was right there with us.

We sat down at the table and the meeting began. As I passed out the proposal, before I could really get started with the presentation, I saw the Director skimming through each page of the proposal that I had just handed him. Once he had made his way to the last page where our offer was, I watched him browse through that page. He then placed the proposal down on the table and looked up at me with an unexpressive look. A bit nervous, I tried to lighten the mood by saying something a little humorous before getting started with the presentation. Unfortunately, that didn't seem to go over very well.

The Director was a nice man and he treated us with extreme kindness, but you could tell that he was a man of business, and that's exactly what he was there for. I continued to proceed forward and started taking the Director through our proposal. I shared with him our passion for people and for ministry. I shared with him a few of the things that we had done in the short amount of time that I had been the Pastor over the church. From visiting and serving people in homeless shelters and juvenile centers, to walking the community and raking leaves for families who were in need of assistance. Even as a small church, we were able to gather donations from stores and businesses to give out Thanksgiving Day baskets to a few families that were in need. We had two incredible sisters in our ministry who really had a passion for helping people, and through their help and assistance we didn't just give those families enough food to last them for one day, but through God's grace we were able to provide a few families with food that could last them for an entire week. We also included some toiletry and household items as often times those are things that family's need as well but are seldom provided. After sharing with him some of the things that we had done in the city, I felt led to just open up and share with him from my heart.

The meeting lasted about 20 minutes, but to me it felt like several hours. At the conclusion of our meeting, The Director (still with an unexpressive look) remained silent for a moment. He then told us in a very calm manner, "we will accept your offer." It took me a few seconds to process what he had just said. I thought to myself, *did I just hear him correctly?* While my mind was still trying to sort through his last words, the Director continued on by telling us that we could connect with his realtor today to receive a purchase agreement for the property.

Now let me stop right here and interject this thought, that if we would have started shouting and praising God like we felt like doing in the Director's office right at that moment, I am fully confident that he would have quickly changed his mind thinking that we had all gone crazy. But in a very calm, civil, and professional way, one by one we discreetly shook the Directors hand, and graciously thanked him for his time. We quietly and discretely walked out of the building as if though nothing had just taken place. But the moment we hit the parking lot, we shouted and praised God like you could never imagine. That parking lot will never be the same.

Later that evening, I had in my hand a signed purchase agreement for the property of an entire former elementary school that sat on close to two acres of land directly in the heart of the city. As I was sitting at home still rejoicing and in awe of God and looking over the signatures at the bottom of the agreement, it was then that reality once again came in and abruptly interrupted this celebratory moment. It slowly begin to dawn on me, that though the district had just accepted our offer..... we didn't have any money.

Though what we had offered the school district was considerably a low amount for purchasing an entire school, it was still a large amount to us. I shared with our congregation that the offer I had given the district had been accepted and the church rejoiced. The church was extremely excited about the possibilities of owning this building, but we all knew that we had an incredible task ahead of us. Since we clearly did not have that kind of money to purchase the facility, I went to a bank in an attempt to get a loan for the amount that we had offered to the district. I took the same proposal that I had presented to the Director with me and met with a Banking Manager. I prayed long and hard that she would see the vision for our ministry, and to my surprise... she did. What a miracle, the Bank Manager was a Christian and we talked extensively about our faith. She thought that the building was an incredible blessing and a great opportunity for our ministry. Though she felt that way, unfortunately the bank did not, and our application was denied. The Bank Manager graciously informed me of the disappointing news but wished our church the very best. One of the last things that she told me before I left her office was, "if it's God's will, it will come to pass." I kindly thanked her for her time and for her encouraging words and headed back to my car.

At this point, we had very limited options as to how to come up with the necessary funds needed in order to purchase this building. The option that was at the top of my list had now just fallen through. We could not get a loan, and we had absolutely no outside help or assistance of any kind from anyone. This was such a great opportunity, but how would we come up with the money that we needed. We had no other choice. If we were going to purchase this property, we would have to raise the money on our own.

With a small congregation of people, we set out on a quest and a mission to raise the amount needed for us to purchase the school building. We started up a giving campaign, and we had a very substantial goal that we needed to reach. I shared with the congregation the amount of money that we would need to raise, and we set a date for a special service where everyone would bring their monetary gifts both large and small, to see how close we could get to our goal. Each family was given an individual amount to try to aspire toward. It was very moving to see the excitement of the people as many were passionate and extremely creative in finding ways to raise their portion to give.

On the day of our major giving campaign, I remember sitting in a back room waiting to go into the service. I was nervous and a bit uneasy as undoubtedly after today, we would know for certain whether or not we would be able to move forward in purchasing that facility. When I came out of the back room into the main area where we had our services, I expected to see our normal crowd of people in the audience excited and ready to give. The truth however is that out of our normal crowd, we were missing quite a few people. Inward nervousness started turning into discouragement, though outwardly I tried my best not to show it. We had been talking about this day for many weeks now, and a lot of people had even verbally told us that they were planning to participate and give, yet on the day when it counted the most, it was only the faithful few that stood to the challenge. Little did I know that the faithful few who attended, came ready to give.

That night, what we were able to raise was nothing short of a miracle. It was not a forced type of giving either, it was such an atmosphere of excitement and celebration that filled that room. By the time the service had concluded, though we had not raised the entire amount needed in order to purchase the facility, I knew in my heart that we could raise the remaining balance by the time we needed it to be raised. There was such an excitement in the eyes of the members that day. Hope was beginning to be revived in the ministry once again. It was a feeling of accomplishment as everyone worked together and extremely hard to do their part in making sure that this vision became a reality. The members remained determined to continue to do whatever was necessary for us to acquire that building.

You know it's something when you have a bread breaking moment with the Master. That's when God takes the very little that you have, and somehow, and in some way stretches it to not only meet your need, but often times to exceed them. By God's grace and with God's favor, throughout that year we were able to raise the total amount needed to purchase that facility through the giving of our faithful congregation alone. No one from the outside helped us or financially supported us in any way to help us purchase the building. It was only through God's grace and through the faithful support of a small congregation that was dedicated and determined to support the vision, that our goal was reached.

On the day of our closing, I remember walking into the title company trying hard to hold back my tears. They were tears of joy as I had a certified check in my hand that was made out for the exact amount of money that we needed to purchase the property. Now as I look back through the process, I have discovered that many times what seemed like a closed door was actually God setting us up for something even greater. When we were declined from receiving a loan from the bank, it was tremendously devastating. But if that bank would have given us the loan, we would have been paying on a monthly mortgage with an extremely high interest rate for many years to come. But here I was, sitting across the table from a representative of the school district at a title company, with a check in my hand for the entire amount of money that we needed in order to purchase the facility. Sometimes you have to go back through your life and thank God not only for the doors that He opened, but also thank Him for the doors that He closed. It may have been disappointing at the moment, but later when you look back throughout your journey, you will soon discover that God had an even greater plan set for your life. Every "no" is not always a setback, sometimes it's a setup, and we have got to learn how to trust God in those hard and disappointing times.

It is still an amazing thought to me, that before we had ever stepped foot into our new facility to have our first service, the building was completely paid off in full. What an incredible blessing and a miracle from God. There are people to this day who have visited our church, and after seeing the building that God has blessed us with, still find it hard to believe that we were able to acquire and pay it off in full without any outside help or assistance. Our response to them has been and will always be the same, nobody can take the credit or the glory for what has taken place, but God.

After we had signed the papers, my wife began looking over the documents discovering something quite ironically unique. She brought me the signed documents and told me to look at the date. We both sat there in utter amazement as our signing and closing date was one year later on the exact same date of our Pastoral Installation service. It is important to note that we did not plan for that, nor did we even realize that the date was the same until later that evening. A year ago that same day, I was sitting in front of a church being installed as a Senior Pastor, wondering what the fate and the future of our ministry was going to be. Now here we were, on that exact same date one year later, being handed the keys to an entire elementary school that now belonged to our church, and the building was completely paid off in full. What an incredible miracle from God.

MOVE IN CELEBRATION

Once we had acquired the property, there was still some work that needed to be done in order to get the facility ready for us to move in. Along with having many classrooms and office space available, the school building also had an elementary size gymnasium where we would soon be holding our services. I remember after getting the facility ready for use, I called Pastor Marvin and informed him that we had received clearance from the city for us to be able to have our services in the new building. I also shared with him that we were planning on having our "Move In Celebration Service" coming soon. He told me that they were excited for us, and that he wanted to come down and be a part of the celebration. He told me that he was planning on bringing their church down to help support us. He told me that they knew firsthand how expensive it can be to move into a new facility, and that they were coming down to be a financial blessing to the ministry. I must say that it felt good to hear Pastor Marvin express that he was proud of us, and it was also a blessing to know that they were planning on coming down to support us as well. Even though we had been placed in a very rocky situation from the launch of this ministry, we still loved them very dearly and there was still something inside of us that really wanted to make Pastor Marvin and Pastor MaLinda both proud.

When Pastor Marvin had originally made the announcement that they were going to install me as the Pastor over the Battle Creek church, he had also announced that they were going to give our ministry some chairs to go along with the building that they were intending to give us. I asked them since our church had now acquired a facility of our own, if they would still be willing to give us the chairs that they had originally promised us. Though they didn't give us the chairs promised, they did give us some chairs that would help us to be able to get by, and we were extremely grateful.

It was starting to feel like things were beginning to come together. Though this was a really great time for the ministry, it was still a very challenging time for my family and I. We were still commuting back and forth from Grand Rapids every week and still living at my parent's home. With the transportation being cut, it left us trying desperately to use our car to commute down sometimes several times a week to and from Battle Creek. The problem was, our vehicle was not at all in the best shape, and on many occasions we would have to use my father's car to transport ourselves to the Battle Creek Church. We were also in the middle of a Winter season, and Winter seasons in Michigan can be very unpredictable. Trying to commute back and forth when there were snow storms certainly made our traveling even more of a challenge at times, so to hear Pastor Marvin say that they were coming down to support the ministry really meant a whole lot to us.

We started getting the facility ready for what we called the "Move In Celebration." During that time, Pastor Marvin and the Grand Rapids church were also having their services in a much larger gym on their ministry campus. I had brothers from the church paint our gymnasium in a way that would incorporate the same type of look and feel of the Grand Rapids Lighthouse church, just with a different color scheme and on a much smaller scale. We made sure that every person that was serving on that day was in uniform and that they were ready to serve in excellence. Daddy was coming home, and I wanted to make sure that everything was just right.

The day had now come for the celebration and my wife and I were extremely excited. The gym was packed from the front to the back. Everyone was in position and everything looked great. I remember before Pastor Marvin arrived, wanting to run downstairs one last time just to make sure that everything and everybody was in place. My wife stopped me and encouraged me to relax, assuring me that everyone was in position and that everything was going to be just fine. Though we were blessed with a gymnasium, it was a smaller gym because the building was a former elementary school. We were very limited on the amount of people that we could fit in the gym, and the room filled up to capacity before the service had even started. In fact, we unfortunately had to turn away many people from the celebration on that day.

When Pastor Marvin arrived, he arrived a little late so we didn't get an opportunity to speak to him before the service. We showed him a portion of the building as we were walking toward the gym for the celebration. The worship experience was amazing, and the presence of God was in the building. The City Commissioner of our district came and presented us with a welcome proclamation from the city. It was absolutely an amazing moment for our ministry.

Now I must stop here for a moment and interject this thought before proceeding further to make sure that my heart is understood. I truly pray that what I'm about to write here is not misinterpreted or read into the wrong way. My prayer is that it would be understood and received in the heart that it is being written.

As the service progressed, we had now come to the time for the offering. Pastor Marvin facilitated the offering portion of the service. He mentioned to those in attendance how proud he was of my wife and I, and how proud he was of the ministry. He said that he wanted to be a blessing to our church, and that he was going to personally sow a love seed that afternoon into our ministry of one hundred dollars. Now let me stop for a moment and be emphatically clear that my wife and I are not at all about money. We were extremely grateful to receive any kind of help and support that he or anyone else was willing to sow into our ministry. But what hurt us that evening was the fact that a local Pastor in the city of Battle Creek, sowed in that same offering, five times as much as our own spiritual father had sown into us that day. The offering for that entire evening was low. In fact, the following week with less people in attendance we had received a greater offering than what we had received during the celebration service itself. Sometimes people are under a false misconception that larger crowds always produce large offerings. But let me take a moment to dispel that thought, as just because people show up for a service or an event, does not mean that people will always support and give.

After the service had concluded, I didn't get a chance to speak to Pastor Marvin personally as from what I was told, he had to quickly leave out to head to another ministry engagement.

What do you do when you think that help is on the way, when you think that a moment of relief is upon you, only to discover that you've got more of the journey left to endure. That night driving back to Grand Rapids, my wife and I just began to encourage each other. We were hurt and a bit disappointed, but deep down inside, we knew that God hadn't brought us this far to allow us to sink here.

Sink Or Swim

CHAPTER SEVEN

SHORE IN THE DISTANCE

That next year was an extremely hard and a very challenging year for us. Being a Pastor by itself can be a stressful task. Counseling people, making sure that departments and auxiliaries are running smoothly, laying before God trying to get a fresh word for bible studies and Sunday services every week. This is only a small diluted resume of the things that many Pastors do. Any Pastor who has started a ministry from the ground up will also tell you that in addition to those things, there are times when we have to become the janitor, the sound technician, the handyman, the praise and worship leader (even if you can't sing), the hospitality team, the intercessory prayer coordinator, the welcome committee and the list goes on and on. And if that's not enough, it can also become extremely stressful to wonder if you're going to make the budget every month. Having a new building created new financial responsibilities that we were now experiencing for the very first time. Each month was a never ending rollercoaster ride. Some months we would breeze right through, other months we didn't know how in the world we were going to make it (in that first year we experienced more of the latter then the former), but somehow by God's amazing grace we would always seem to make it through.

Though the ministry was maintaining and even beginning to grow in size, all of this was now starting to take a major toll on my health. I started experiencing extreme chest pains. I would find myself going in and out of the hospital on several occasions trying hard to figure out what was going on with my body. Every time I would go to the hospital, they would send me home with some pain medicine and tell me that everything seemed to be fine. I continued to try and press forward in ministry even though things were really starting to become unbearable and overwhelming. Driving back and forth weekly was really starting to become overtaxing, and at this point there was absolutely nothing that I could do about it.

In an effort to try and bring more growth to the church, and in an attempt to try and reach a different crowd of people, we attempted to add on an additional second service on Sundays. Our ministry started to grow even more with the additional service however, my body was really beginning to feel the effects and the stress. The pain in my chest started to come on more and more frequently and more severe. Other symptoms started to arise as well. My neck started to stiffen up badly and it became extremely challenging for me to be able to turn my head in any direction. I started experiencing real bad dizzy spells which was all accompanied by an extremely painful pressure in my head that I felt around my temple areas.

There were times that I would start seeing white dots or what looked like white stars, and I felt like I was going to pass out. My legs would get extremely weak underneath me, and I would find it hard to remain standing and would have to find a seat quickly. I remember trying to walk around in the grocery store with my wife and I would become so dizzy that I would have to go to the car and wait for her there. I continued to go back and forth to the emergency room trying to figure out what was wrong with me. There were even times when I would be in the emergency room all night long on a Saturday evening. Because we did not have any ministers in operation that I could turn our service over to at the time, I would still get on the road early that Sunday morning to drive down to Battle Creek and preach two services. Our members had no clue that hidden underneath my suit jacket was a hospital band still strapped to my arm.

After all of the examinations and tests, the Doctors still could not find anything wrong with me. They did heart scans and various tests and everything would come back normal. At one point my Doctor wanted to do an MRI on my brain. He wanted to be sure that there was nothing going on in my head that they may have somehow possibly overlooked. I had never had an MRI done on my brain before and I didn't know really what to expect. I asked the nurse who was scheduling my appointment about the MRI process. I was trying my best to enquire and get as much information as I possibly could. She assured me that it was not a bad procedure at all and that I would be absolutely fine.

When the day came for me to receive the MRI, I remember walking down with my wife to the waiting room where the procedure was scheduled to take place. I thought to myself, *this should be a breeze,* as I had done several other tests previously, so really how bad could this one be? The nurse brought my wife and I into an extremely nice looking waiting room. As I was sitting there observing and looking around this beautiful room that had new modern furniture and windows that gave such a natural and beautiful burst of sunlight, I thought to myself, *this is going to be much easier than I thought.* The nurse who was running my MRI scan for that day came out and greeted me. She asked me if I was ready to go, in which I responded "yes." After a small level of preparation, she took me around the corner into a darker room. There was no natural burst of sunlight anywhere to be found in that room. In fact, there were no windows anywhere to be found in that room. It looked like we had taken a wrong turn somewhere and had ended up in an oversized janitors closet. We entered into the dim room, and it had a big machine-like structure with a hole in it. I asked the nurse, "what is that?" She told me that this was the machine that was going to be doing my MRI scan. The nurse then proceeded to explain to me that this was about a thirty minute procedure where they would be taking roughly three pictures total. The first picture would take about twelve minutes, the next picture would take about eight minutes, and the final picture would take about ten minutes. She said if you move while you are in the machine that it can affect the picture being taken. She said if that happens, we may have to start the procedure all over again. The machine had a little circle entrance, and in the middle of the machine your body lays on a small little mat and is inserted head first inside of the machine. It is a very tight space, and she was telling me that I needed to be in there (as well as be very still) for about thirty minutes.

In my mind I started coaching myself, *okay.... I can do this, I can do this.* I started quoting all the motivational scriptures that I could think of at the moment, *God has not given me the spirit of fear, but of power, love, and a sound mind.* My motivation was starting to kick in and take over. I was feeling my confidence stepping up to the plate. This was not going to be that bad. I got down and laid on that small skinny pad waiting to be inserted into the mouth of this machine. The nurse asked me if I was ready to be inserted? I told her, "yes let's do it." It was at that moment that she placed a cage like device around my head. I said, "hold up... wait a second, nobody said anything about a cage thing being around my head." The nurse assured me that everything was safe and that the sooner we started, the sooner the procedure would be over. I thought it through for a second, and then I told the nurse that I needed a moment. She removed the cage like device, and I went out to that nice relaxing waiting area where my wife was sitting enjoying herself very comfortably. When my wife looked up and saw me come out she said, "wow that was fast." I started to explain to her that I had not started the procedure yet, and that I wasn't sure if I could do it. The nurse was gracious enough to allow me to bring my wife into the room to

121

show her the machine. When my wife had seen this mammoth beast of a machine, and saw what I had to go through, she immediately understood what I was feeling. Finally!!! I had someone around here who understood what I was going through. She is bone of my bone and flesh of my flesh and if anyone was going to have my back, I knew it would be her. I was expecting to hear her say something like, *maybe there's another way that we can find out what's going on with you.* With no hesitation I would have totally agreed with her. I needed some words of comfort, some words of hope and encouragement. Or better yet, I needed some words that would provide me with a way of escape. Words like, *we can do this another time honey.* Yes!!! That would have been perfect. But instead, the words that came out of her mouth were..... "you can do this!" ....That wasn't quite the words that I was looking for.

The nurse then advise me that if I wanted to, I could reschedule to do the procedure at a later time under sedation. I thought to myself, *wait, I did not come this far to turn back now.* I looked at the nurse and said to her, "no that's ok, let's do it." My wife went back out to that beautiful, pleasantly relaxing and very comfortable waiting area, and I laid on that small pad once again now awaiting for the procedure to begin. Before inserting me into the machine, the nurse advised me that while the MRI is being done that the machine can get pretty loud. She gave me some headphones and said that they can turn on a radio station of my choice to help elevate some of the noise. She said that the music can also be soothing

122

throughout the process. I put the headphones on and she inserted me into the machine. Talking through the monitor the nurse asked me if there was a radio station that I preferred to listen to. Grand Rapids had a gospel radio station and I told her to place it on that station. She tried to find it but unfortunately she was unable to get it at the moment. The nurse found a different radio station and the procedure began.

I was laying in the machine and it really wasn't all that bad. I was overcoming my fears and the music was actually rather soothing. After about a minute of the music playing, the music went off and the morning news came on. The news report literally went something like this. Four people died last night in an out of control house fire. Two people are now dead and one person is in critical condition from a car accident that took place yesterday. There was a shooting on the south side that left two people in stable condition and one person dead last night. Police are still investigating and the suspect has not yet been found. I'm thinking to myself..... *you have got to be kidding me.... so much for that soothing music.* After the first picture was taken, the nurse came back on the intercom to see how I was doing. I kindly asked her if she could please turn the radio to a different station.

While I was in that machine, no longer in fear, I started looking back throughout my life and I started to question why I was even in that hospital in the first place. Why was I in this situation? As I reminisced back, all I could think of was the many sacrifices that I was making and had made to try and bring this vision to pass. I started to think, *God, I am giving you my all and trying my hardest to serve your people and right now I don't know if I can take much more of this.* It was way too much for me to bare any longer. Right there during my MRI testing, I literally started coming to my breaking point.

It was at that moment, right there in that very tight place that I began to feel the presence and the peace of God come over me. It was as if though God was reassuring me that He was still with me, and that He hadn't brought me this far to leave me. The peace that came over me was a peace that I cannot even begin to describe, and just as I was beginning to fully embrace that moment, the nurse pulled me out of the machine and said, "good job, you're all done." I was thinking to myself, *"wait..... can you put me back in there for about fifteen more minutes."*

It's something when God meets you in tight places. Many times when you go through situations it can seem as if though God is silent. So when He shows up in your most broken condition, you learn to value and cherish every single moment with Him that you possibly can. It reminds me of when Jacob was in distress because he was about to see his brother who he had betrayed for the very first time since he had wronged him. In sheer and utter fear, Jacob finds himself alone. No company to comfort him, no wife to console him, just Jacob living in a tight and painful place. It is here where the bible says that Jacob wrestled with God and refused to let Him go. To be honest with you, I don't blame him. Those unique moments when God shows up Himself in your most painful place, you don't ever want to let Him go. After being blessed by God, the bible says in Genesis 32:30, *And Jacob called the name of the place Peniel: For I have seen God face to face.* One biblical help-study to this text suggests that though the word Peniel is known as the "Face of God," another way to look at this in retrospect to Jacobs experience, is to actually view the word as "Facing God." It is because you cannot see the face of God, unless you are truly facing Him. Jacob's encounter forced him to take his focus off of his painful circumstance and caused him to literally have to face God, and here I was for the last thirty minutes lying inside a machine facing up. It was almost as if though God was saying, I brought you to this tight uncomfortable place, away from all of your family, friends, and away from all of your problems, to force you to take your eyes off of your situation - and if only but for a moment, I had to cause you to face Me. That day I left the hospital not with a reassurance that my situation was going to get any better, but rather I left the hospital that day with something even greater, the reassurance that God was still with me.

VACATION

Later I shared with our congregation a testimony of how I had been back and forth to the hospital and the word began to spread. After hearing about it, I received a call from Pastor Marvin and we talked briefly about how I had been in and out of the hospital. He then told me that he wanted to come down to one of our services to be with us on a Sunday afternoon. We were able to place a date on the calendar, and it was not to long there after that the date arrived. For this particular visit, not only did Pastor Marvin come down to be with us that afternoon, but Pastor MaLinda had also come down as well. This was a very unique and a very special moment for my wife and I. We were truly thankful that Pastor MaLinda had come down to be with us that day. It really touched our hearts in a very special way to have her presence with us.

Before Pastor Marvin spoke that afternoon, Pastor MaLinda took a moment to share a few words with our congregation. In her remarks, she took that time to really encourage my wife. She began to share and express to us all, that ministry is not at all easy. She said to our congregation that she needed their word that my wife will never cry a tear that they won't catch before it hits the ground - that my wife will never pray alone, and that she will never have to worry about covering her children by herself while she is on the vision field. She told them to honor her, respect her, serve her, do not envy at her and not to get in the way of the vision that God has for her. She then encouraged our congregation to do something special for my wife, adding that she was coming back down with her women to celebrate my wife with us. This was an incredibly touching moment for my wife.

For many years I watched my wife feel inadequate and ill-equipped for the task that God had given her as becoming a First Lady. I don't know if there is an official First Lady's job description, or if there is an official First

Lady manual that lists the responsibilities that First Lady's do. And depending on who you may ask, I am beyond confident that you will receive many varying opinions and views on the topic of what people feel a First Lady's role in the church should be. Even television has now recently jumped on board trying to give us their rendition of what varying First Lady roles can look like.

I cannot speak for how everyone else may interpret the role of a First Lady, but I can tell you a few things that I have discovered that seem to be universal concerning what many Pastor's wives tend to go through. One thing is the fact that First Lady's are attached and connected to the Pastor of the church. Now I know that this is an obvious observation, but there are some underlining challenges that come along with this connection. This means that often times the Pastor's wife has to give encouragement to the one who encourages everyone else. When members in our congregation get weak, they come to the Pastor for encouragement. But when Pastors get weak and weary, most of the times their congregations may never even know it. There is however one person who not only sees the burden, but also directly feels and is affected by that burden, and that person is the Pastor's wife. She often hears his frustrations and she often feels his pain. That in and of itself can be an overwhelming pressure for many First Ladies to have to handle. Add this to the fact that most First Ladies have to share their husbands with so many people, and that ministry can become a never ending ongoing perpetual cycle. Some people actually think that when we say amen at the end of a Sunday service that ministry actually ends... but that is completely far from the truth. Ministry can evolve itself to become a continual list of ongoing things to accomplish, goals to be met, and things to be done. Schedules, meetings, consultations and plans can easily grow to become completely out of control. This can cause a Pastor to start placing ministry responsibilities before their families which can also become a great potential danger to a marriage.

Along with all of this, often times various women in the church may desire to glean from the First Lady or even receive mentorship from her. There are some who desire to have a First Lady in whom they can confide in, share and receive encouraging words pertaining to their own personal struggles in life. Then there are those who want their Pastor's wife to not only be their First Lady, but to also be their BFF (Best Friend Forever). Individuals like this want an exclusively close relationship with their First Lady. They want to do things with the First Lady, they want to hang out with the First Lady, and the First Lady must always make it a priority to respond back to their text messages within a 15 second ratio, or the whole world is coming to an end (I say that part jokingly, but there is certainly a level of truth to it). Even if a Pastor's wife does desire to have a close friendship with an individual in their congregation, that relationship typically tends to become one-sided in nature. It is because the individual may be able to share their deepest struggles with their First Lady, but often times the First Lady is unable to share their deepest struggles (whether concerning her

128

husband, the church, her family, or even concerning her own personal issues) with that individual. Reasons why this can be so challenging can stem from trust related issues to even a potential conflict of interest. Some Pastor's wives may actually have been able to find a balance or a true friendship within their congregation in which they can confide in, but honestly, those relationships are extremely rare and often times can tend to potentially back fire at some point in the relationship.

Most First Ladies would benefit from developing friendships outside of the church with other First Lady's who really know and understand the struggles that they both face. But even finding healthy relationships among fellow Pastor's wives can be a very difficult challenge. Most First Lady's really don't have people that they can truly talk to or confide in for help and encouragement for themselves. It can be extremely challenging for them to really find trustworthy friendships, making it a very lonely road for most Pastor's wives. If all of this were not enough, for those First Ladies who have children, they have to somehow manage the responsibilities of being a mother, wife, and a First Lady all at the same time. These things alone really have the potential to bring about a great level of pressure, and often times can develop into an even greater level of discouragement and frustration. Being a Pastor's wife can be much more challenging than many people may think.

After the announcement was made that I would be the Pastor over the Battle Creek church, my wife desired to receive some help to try and learn and prepare for this new role that she would soon be walking into as a Pastor's wife. She also had a passionate desire to get some help on becoming a stronger woman of God in general. All of these components would certainly be much needed for the assignment and for the task that lied directly ahead. Though this was something that my wife truly desired, it was something that she unfortunately did not receive. When my wife requested help and assistance in those areas, she was advised to meet with another woman of God who was a minister at the Grand Rapids church location during that time. My wife greatly appreciated those meetings and the sessions were great however, they only met together on a few short occasions.

When we were later placed over the Battle Creek church, as I mentioned earlier, I watched my wife really struggle for several years trying to find and discover herself and her role. The pressures that were resting on me, our children, and our church were now also starting to take a toll on her. So when Pastor MaLinda began to encourage her that night, that was a very special moment for her.

On that evening, Pastor Marvin and Pastor MaLinda also announced that they desired to give my family and I some rest from our ministry responsibilities, and that they were going to send us away for an all expense paid trip to Florida for a week. I don't think I have ever seen my kids light up the way they did that night. It was absolutely a blessing to know that a getaway was in our near future. Just to be able to relax and not have to worry about the stress of taking care of a church was needed for us majorly in that season. This would be our first real vacation together as a family EVER, and we were excited and extremely thankful to them both for this opportunity.

That night's service was an incredible evening. Once again, everything was really beginning to feel like it was all starting to come together. From the time that we had first been launched out, there seemed to be such a distance between us. Don't get me wrong, we would speak to Pastor Marvin and Pastor MaLinda on occasion, but there really seemed to be a barrier that was present. But for the first time that night since I had been released as the Pastor over the Battle Creek church, it really felt like there was a true connection starting to be restored.

We were very thankful for the trip that they were sending us on, but truthfully and honesty speaking, it was their presence that night that was the greatest gift. Words can't even begin to describe how my wife and I felt just having them both present with us that evening. The feeling of support and affirmation was incredible, and it was something that my wife and I had longed for. Up to this point, we felt like we had been going through this journey by ourselves, and having them present with us that evening, touched our lives more than they will ever know. In spite of everything that we had endured, we still loved Pastor Marvin and Pastor MaLinda very dearly. We had been giving everything that we had (literally) trying to keep a ministry that they had originally launched and started alive, and we were also trying to somehow and in some way make them both proud.

That night after the service had ended, I remember Pastor MaLinda coming out of my office. She came out and stood next to the stairwell that led down to the area where they had parked. She gave me a hug and looked at me and said, "We are very proud of you man of God." Now I had heard Pastor MaLinda tell us that before, but on that night, to me there was something different about it. I told her thank you and that we loved her, and then I watched her go down the steps with Pastor Marvin and another gentleman who had come along with them.

My wife and I celebrated that evening. We were extremely thankful unto God for what had taken place. And the promise that Pastor Marvin and Pastor MaLinda had made to send our family away to Florida, they absolutely kept their word. Pastor MaLinda worked extremely hard and overtime to make sure that my family and I went on that vacation. Our flights had been scheduled, everything had been set up, and we were getting packed and ready to go. But as we were preparing for our trip, my wife was contacted by someone from the Grand Rapids church, and asked if she could design a flyer for a conference call prayer-line that was being set up on Pastor MaLinda's behalf.

Approximately a year or so prior to this moment, It was announced that Pastor MaLinda had been diagnosed with colon cancer. Everyone was in great prayer for her during that very challenging season of her life, and amazingly by God's grace and power she received a report from the Doctor that the cancer was gone and that she was completely cancer free. It was an incredible miracle. We all celebrated with her the news of her remarkable recovery. But now almost a half a year later, we were being told that the cancer was now trying to resurface itself, and my wife was being asked to create a flyer to help solicit prayers from people from around the country on Pastor MaLinda's behalf. On the day that we flew out of town to Florida, my wife designed a flyer right before we had left, and sent it to the person who had requested it.

Though we had received the information that the cancer was somehow trying to resurface itself, we did not believe that Pastor MaLinda's condition was as detrimentally severe. It was because just a few weeks earlier she was with us at our church. She was strong, beautiful, and as vibrant as ever. She carried with her that confident "Super-Natural Sista" presence that seemed to accompany her every time she would enter into a room. In the last couple of days, we had even gone back and forth through e-mail with her, and all throughout our interactions and correspondences everything was very much upbeat. There was absolutely no hint or sign to us that anything even remotely close to severe was taking place. My wife and I believed strongly that just like the last time, whatever was trying to resurface itself - through God's power, it would soon be completely gone once again.

We made our way to the airport that day and found ourselves on a flight headed down to sunny Orlando Florida. It was an amazing trip. I was able to get some much needed rest, our kids had an incredible time, and my wife and I had gotten an opportunity to spend some quality time with each other. Our family and I had NEVER had a vacation like this together EVER! It was an extremely blessed experience for us all.

While we were in Florida, on occasion I would slip away into our room and spend some time with God in prayer. I thanked Him for the Sapp family who had blessed us with this trip. While in prayer, God began to share with me in that room, that when you are faithful to His will, and when you are not weary in well doing, that you will reap if you faint not. While looking out of the window at the beautiful Florida view that was filled with palm trees and a sunrise that was absolutely amazing, I felt God impress upon me that this was where our journey was about to shift. God shared with me that morning that things were now about to start changing in our lives, but that there was still yet more opposition to endure. The road ahead would still have its challenges, but many of our hardest obstacles that we were currently facing was now about to start coming to an end. God's presence encouraged and filled my spirit that day, and I was extremely grateful to Him. The last time I had felt His presence like that, I was in a very tight place. But here I was in a beautiful place now, and God was assuring me that everything was going to be ok. I told God that morning that I was ready for whatever the road ahead may bring our way, and I thanked God for keeping us throughout our journey. We had hit some extremely hard times, but God had revealed Himself to us in so many different ways, and I thanked Him for not letting us drown.

I want to take a moment to encourage those of you who are living in a "turning point" moment in your life. Turning points are very unique moments. They are unique because though it may be a turning point in your life, things around you may still be very much in great disarray. It is because God often begins a turning point within us, before it ever begins to manifest outside of us. Though turmoil may still be going on around you, you can sense within your heart that something is about to shift and change for the better. You recognize clearly that God is up to something on your behalf, it's just that it has not fully manifested yet. Turning points in your life can also cause you to handle situations much differently. Things that would normally hurt you, discourage you, or even disappoint you, no longer have the same kind of effect on you. Don't get me wrong, those circumstances can still hurt, it's just that you realize you are no longer simply moving through it, you are now moving out of it. It's like you can see an exit sign in a clouded distance, and even though it may still be extremely far away, your just happy to see an exit sign. For me, in the midst of being in water for so long, for the first time in a very long time..... I saw land. It was still far away, but nevertheless, I saw it.

Turning points are indeed incredible moments. It's the unlocking of the prison door by the messenger that was sent in the book of Genesis to get Joseph out of jail. Joseph was still in the prison, but he was on his way out of it. He still had quite a journey ahead of him, as he would have to trust and rely on God to interpret the Pharaohs dream. And even if God came through for him in that way, Joseph still had absolutely no clue what God had in store for his future. All Joseph knew, was that he was coming out of prison while he was still standing inside of it. For those of you who are in your season of turnaround, whatever you do, **don't you dare give up!!** You may be standing in it, but by God's grace soon you will be coming out of it. If you made it through all of the obstacles of your past and you can see your destiny in the distance, with God's help, you can surely make it to the very end.

God really encouraged my heart while we were on that Florida trip. I felt revitalized both spiritually and physically. I knew that there were still some obstacles ahead that we would have to endure, but with all of the confirmation that God was giving me (from that tight place in the hospital room, to the beautiful place in our Florida room), I knew that everything was going to be okay.

When we got back home, we thanked Pastor Marvin and Pastor MaLinda for sending us down to Florida. We were extremely grateful, and above all things we were thankful to now sense what felt like a reconnection happening between us and between our ministries. Pastor MaLinda e-mailed back, encouraging us once again of how proud they were of my wife and I.

I cannot even begin to describe to you the joy my wife and I felt. On the night that Pastor MaLinda had come down to our church, she shared with us that she was coming back down with her women to celebrate and be with my wife. My wife was very excited to soon be able to connect with Pastor MaLinda to receive (if nothing more) some encouragement and simply just some time together. My wife had never had anyone that had taken the time to really pour into her, and that was something that she really truly desired. So just knowing that she was about to spend even just a little time with Pastor MaLinda in this season of our lives made my wife ecstatic. She was also extremely happy about having Pastor MaLinda and the Super Natural Sista's come down to the Battle Creek church to fellowship with us. When Pastor MaLinda had announced that she was coming back down with her women, my wife completely lit up. She started looking over dates trying to get things ready and set for them to come down. She really wanted to go all out to show them love, pamper them, and to really try and build that connection. My wife began working overtime trying to set up things for Pastor MaLinda and our Grand Rapids Super Natural Sista's to come down and fellowship together with us.

At this time, the weekly conference call prayer-line was still taking place for Pastor MaLinda. One of the individuals in charge of the conference call asked me if I would be willing to be one of the individuals to pray on the conference line for Pastor MaLinda during a few of the prayer sessions.

Without any hesitation I said that I would do it, as we were truly believing God for a divine miracle on her behalf.

My wife and I along with many others, did not know Pastor MaLinda's true condition. I am sure that only a very carefully hand-selected few, may have truly been informed of how severe her condition was becoming. To many of us, the last image that we had seen of Pastor MaLinda was of a strong vibrant woman, and though we all took this situation very seriously, we would have never expected the inevitable.

A couple weeks later, I had a meeting with a Pastor friend of mine at a restaurant in Grand Rapids. When I got home from that meeting, I realized that I had left my wallet at the place where we had met that morning, so I drove back to get my wallet. When I pulled up to the restaurant, I received a phone call and an individual on the other line began to encourage me as if though something had taken place. They said that they had heard that Pastor MaLinda had passed away but that they wanted to confirm with me if it was true or not. I immediately hung up the phone and called my wife to see if she had heard anything. She said that she did not know of anything, but that she was going to call someone to see if it was true or not.

My wife called one of the individuals that was on the Grand Rapids Church board and within minutes, my phone rang again. When I picked up the phone, all I could hear was weeping in the background. My wife could not say a single word. It was then that I knew that this was not at all a rumor, it was reality. As my wife began to gather some strength to try and speak, she verbally confirmed to me what I already knew from the moment I had answered that call. I hung up the phone and I sat in the parking lot of that restaurant in tears and in utter disbelief. It was absolutely impossible.... it could not be true. She was just with us at our church less than two months ago. She had just worked extensively hard, going completely out of her way to make sure that my family and I went on that vacation... it could not be true. That whole day was completely unreal.

This hit my wife and I extremely hard. In spite of all we had been through, we still loved Pastor Marvin and Pastor MaLinda both very dearly. Even to this very day, we love them both very much. That is one of the reasons why we continued to push so hard to build their ministry. From their youth department years ago, to the college ministry, and even now to the Battle Creek Church, we would always give our all. First because we wanted to please God, and secondly because we truly loved them and wanted to see their vision come to pass.

It was also very painful for me because honestly speaking, I had more of a relationship with Pastor MaLinda than I did with Pastor Marvin, as we would meet more often. Though I love Pastor Marvin dearly to this very day, his key signature phrase pertaining to how he mentored me, is that he mentored me from a distance. I must honestly and respectably say, that the latter portion of that phrase is absolutely true. There has always been a great level of distance between Pastor Marvin and I, even in the area of mentorship. And that distance would prove to find its way also between our churches. Pastor MaLinda was for the most part the glue that somehow kept things cohesively together. Even though there was not the greatest connection between us, it was often her efforts that would somehow keep things connected. She was the communicator and often times the balancer..... but now, in just a moments time, she was gone. And that reconnection (that we had felt earlier) and our relationship with our Overseer, would now start to become distant once again.

Sink Or Swim

CHAPTER EIGHT

THE MASTER OF THE SEA

We were now going on our third year of ministry and my family and I were still unable to move to the city of Battle Creek. The church was now starting to financially get on its feet, especially with the fact that we were now beginning to adjust to the additional expenses of having a school building that needed to be maintained.

Throughout this entire process, my natural father and mother were extremely gracious to our family. I say this with absolutely no hint of reservation, that if it had not been for them, there would have been no Lighthouse Battle Creek. They allowed my wife, my three boys, along with myself to live with them not just for a couple of months, but rather for several years while we were working extensively hard to try and build the Battle Creek church.

As I've mentioned before, my father would often times allow us to use his vehicle to be able to drive back and forth to the Battle Creek church because our car was not in the best condition to make the trip. Being on the road back and forth, especially as extensively as we were was not at all good for our children. Our kids were still enrolled in school in Grand Rapids, so it was very important to my wife and I that we did not have them arriving home at extremely late hours of the night. My mother would help watch our children almost every time we would need to travel to Battle Creek for services. She would cook them meals and make sure that they were tucked in bed for school the next morning.

There were many times that I would feel like quitting and giving up, but my father would always encourage me and tell me, "you can do it son." I even remember times that we would visit special events that would be taking place at the Grand Rapids church location to come out and show our love and support. Because we didn't have much, my father would give my wife and I some money, and would tell us to go and pick out a nice outfit for the both of us. Even though we were going through some very challenging and rough times, from the outside looking in, it appeared that we were doing okay. My father would always encourage us to hold our heads up high. He would always remind us that we were children of God and that our service was not unto man, but that it was unto God and Him alone.

My Father and Mother have done so much for us, and they would always go beyond the call of duty to make sure that our family was taken care of. I remember one Christmas my wife and I did not have any money to our name. Our kids woke up that morning to find presents underneath the

Christmas tree signed from mommy and daddy. I'm sure you can imagine our children's reaction when they discovered presents underneath the tree. I was thinking to myself, *we never bought any Christmas presents.* And the truth of the matter was, we didn't. My parents had gone out and purchased some gifts on our behalf to give to our children. You can't even begin to imagine what my heart was feeling at that moment. To see the excitement of my children was priceless. But though it was a blessing to see the smiles and laughter resonating from my boys after each opened gift, and though it was such a blessing to receive the "big-squeezy" hugs of gratitude that soon followed, it was also challenging for me to watch my mother and father doing what they could to help our family. Though my parents had a heart to bless us, they were far from financially well off. They had their own bills to pay, and everything that they were doing for us was a sacrifice for them to do. I was extremely grateful for their support, but at the same time my heart hurt deeply because my parents were sacrificing so much for us to be able to survive.

After three years of living with my parents, one day my father came up to me and said, "son, we need to talk." You could hear the seriousness in his voice and you could tell that what he wanted to discuss with me was important. That day my father said something to me that I will never forget. He said to me, "I'm sorry son, but you can no longer live here with your mom and I." My heart sunk when I heard him say those words, but I knew that what he was speaking was right. They had helped us for so long, and they could not continue to help us like this. I was working very hard trying to get the ministry to the level where it could support us, and though we were getting very close, we were still not quite where we needed to be. With us adding on the second service, it brought about a substantial level of increase where the church was doing well. It was really looking as if though we would finally be able to make the transition to the city. But when my health began to fade, I had to let the second service go. We were getting extremely close to being able to transition, but we simply were not quite there yet. When my father shared with me that we could no longer stay with them, my mind immediately started racing trying to figure out what our families next move needed to be. I wasn't quite sure exactly what we were going to do next, but I knew for certain that something would have to be done quickly. I couldn't blame my father at all for saying what he had said to me. In fact I completely understood. I knew without a shadow of a doubt that he was speaking this to me completely out of love. It had been three years that they had supported and had placed a roof over our heads, providing for us in so many different ways. Now my natural father stood face to face with his son, discerning clearly that the time had come for us to make our transitional separation. Though I understood and agreed with his decision totally, the question in my mind was, *what are we going to do now?* Before I was able to respond back to what my father had said to me, he continued speaking. He told me, "your church needs you in Battle Creek, not here." He said, "this is what we're going to do." He told me to go down to Battle Creek and to look for an apartment that was big enough to house his daughter, his three grandchildren, and myself. He said, "when you find a place that is suitable for you and your family, your mother and I are going to take care of your rent every month for the next eight months to a year." He told me, "with you being in the city, and with you being able to operate fully as the Pastor, by the end of that time the church should be at a level where it is able to take care of you and your family from there."

It is still very emotional for me to even reminisce back to this moment. To know that the way my family and I finally became settled in the city of Battle Creek Michigan, was because my natural father and mother made a decision to financially help us, to ensure that their son was properly relocated to the city. No words can even begin to come remotely close to describing how I felt at that moment. It was a mixture of excitement but extreme hurt all at the same time. I was hurt because this was not at all my father and mother's responsibility to relocate my family. They should have been using their money to enjoy their own life, yet they chose to unselfishly pour into ours. On the other hand, I was excited because I knew that moving down to the city would alleviate an insurmountable level of stress. We would be able to get settled and finally have a place that we could call home again. I told my father that one day I was going to pay them back for everything that both he and my mother had ever done for us. He looked at me and responded, "no need son, you just succeeding in what God has called you to do, is pay back enough for me."

MOVE IN TO OUR APARTMENT

My wife and I went on a search and we found a nice three bedroom apartment in Battle Creek. When we finally moved and got settled in, just looking at my wife's face you could see such a glow. The excitement of having our own place again was overwhelming. This was the very first time that we had a place to call home since we had lost our house several years earlier. I didn't know what to do with myself. We could go up to the church anytime we wanted to without having to drive an hour and ten minutes there and back. We were also extremely excited for our children. Now that we had moved to Battle Creek, my wife and I were able to spend more time with them. We were also happy to get our kids settled and enrolled in school in the city.

Our presence of moving to Battle Creek had a major impact on our church as well. We started to gain some great momentum in the ministry as I was now able to truly focus on the church. I was more available for counseling sessions, leadership guidance, as well as many other very important and essential things. It was an unbelievable moment. After a couple of years of being installed as the Senior Pastor of the Battle Creek church, we were finally now getting settled into the city. Though my parents had said that they were willing to take care of our rent and help our family for the next eight months to a year, I wanted to work as hard as I could to try and elevate the burden from off of my parents much sooner than that. I knew that it was possible, but I also knew that it would definitely take some work. Running and managing an entire school building has its expenses, especially in the winter months as the school's heating system was ran from an older boiler unit. There are certainly other expenses that come along with running a school building as well. Regardless of this, I knew that with God it was possible for us to reach our goal.

At the very beginning stages of the church when Lighthouse Battle Creek had first opened up, there was a couple who would visit the church and had eventually joined the ministry long before my wife and I had ever arrived. After attending for a while, the gentleman's wife became pregnant, and after giving birth to their child they begin to step away from the ministry for a while. When they made a decision to step away, that is when my wife and I started coming down to the Battle Creek Church to start helping out with the ministry. Our paths had never crossed, we had never met, nor had we ever seen each other before. While assisting the Battle Creek church and even after becoming installed as the Senior Pastor over the church, I had been hearing a great deal about this gentleman and about his family.

One day I felt led to reach out to him, and I contacted him via Facebook. Through a Facebook message, I introduced myself and also invited him to come out and be a part of a special program that our church was running for an entire month called August Awareness Month. It was a program were we were trying to help bring resources and information to the community, helping them to better understand the importance of health, hygiene, education, and proper financial management. The gentleman and I had never spoken before, and I wasn't quite sure exactly how he would respond back to the invitation. But to my surprise, he responded back and told me that he would be honored to come out to the program. From that moment on, he and his family began revisiting the church, and after getting reacquainted with the ministry again, they later made a decision to officially rejoin the church.

One evening, I received a Facebook message from that gentleman, and in his message he began to encourage my wife and I concerning our recent transition to the city. He nor his wife (or anyone from the Battle Creek church for that matter) knew of the situation surrounding what my family and I had to endure to move to the city. In that inbox message, he told me that he wasn't quite sure what it was, but that both him and his wife felt a passion to help assist my family and I during this transitional season of our lives. He told me that they owned a home, but that they were in the process of actually purchasing a new house for themselves. He told me that opposed to selling their current place, they felt led to see if we would be interested in renting out their former home from them. He said that he was pretty sure that the place that they were offering would provide us with much more living space for our family, than the apartment that we were currently living in. He said if we were interested and would like to take a look at the place, to let him know and maybe we could work something out.

Though this sounded like an incredible opportunity, my wife and I had just gotten settled and unpacked into our new apartment. Truthfully speaking, we really loved our place as it was a very nice size apartment for our family. The kids had their own room together and it was very spacious, my wife and I had our own bedroom that was very nice in size. I also had my own office, and we had a beautiful kitchen and two nice sized bathrooms (those parts were more important to my wife then myself). We also had a very spacious family room. Honestly, there was really no need for us to move. Especially with the thought of having to repack boxes and move furniture again. That was something that we did not at all desire to do. If repacking boxes wasn't enough of a defusing element to our consideration, we lived on the third floor of our apartment complex. Getting our furniture up three flights of long stairs was already quite the challenge, we could only imagine what it would be like trying to get everything back down those same flights of stairs once again. My wife and I talked things over between ourselves and we were pretty set on staying at our apartment. We did however make a decision to at least go and look at their place as they did not have to be courteous and reach out to us in that manner. The fact that they had even thought about us in that way, in our heart seemed to at least merit a respectful visit.

We set up a day to do a walk through, and when that day arrived my wife was unfortunately unable to make it. That left me as the family representative for us all. When I walked in, the place was amazing and absolutely beautiful. It had a newer modern look, and it was a very spacious home with so many great features. It also had a garage and a beautiful large finished basement with plenty of room for the kids to be able to play and run around. After viewing the property, I went back home and shared with my wife how beautiful the place was. I began to share with her that with the added space for the kids in the basement alone, it may be worth us repacking everything and conquering those three flights of long steps once again. We set up another appointment for us to go through the house, and this time my wife and children came along with me. The moment they walked through the door, they all fell in love with the place immediately.

I contact the gentleman back and I let him know that we were definitely interested and would love to talk further about what their desires where for the home, and what moving forward would possibly look like. The gentleman responded back expressing his excitement to hear that we were interested. In that message, he began sharing with me the amount of money that they were paying monthly for their home. He expressed to me that if we were able to pay the same amount that they were paying monthly for the place, we could certainly move forward. After reading that inbox message, I knew right then and there that we would not be able to move into that home. Their mortgage payment alone was almost double the amount that we were paying for our three bedroom apartment, and that did not even include the additional cost of adding their utilities. It was no way in the world that we would be able to afford to pay that kind of money. We were working hard just to try and get the church at a level where it could soon be able to compensate our family for just our apartment. As beautiful as their home was, it was simply way too far out of our reach financially for my wife and I to be able to afford.

A little disappointed yet completely content, I sent a message back to the gentleman and told him that we could not afford the amount that they were asking for. I told him that honestly all we could afford was the amount that we were currently paying for our apartment at the moment. I told him that I could try and see if we could stretch a little further, but that honestly it would be such a major stretch for us, as what we were currently paying was a major leap of faith for us already. I told him that we did not want to get in their way, as they could easily rent out their home (especially as beautiful as it was) to someone who could actually afford the amount that they were looking for. The gentleman responded back, and this is the message response that he sent me.

> "I honestly love your humbleness Pastor. And I appreciate the
> fact you're looking at the situation from my perspective. But this
> is not about me or how much I can get but more about me doing
> what I'm asked to do. The door is opened for me to bless you
> and your family. You will not need to pay no more than your
> current situation including utilities. This is not about money it's
> about you being willing to walk and move when God ask you to
> move. Your act of faith to move to Battle Creek says so much

about your dedication to God. And this is just a chip of the iceberg of what God has in store for your faithfulness."

After reading that inbox message, I did not know how to respond. My wife and I were absolutely speechless. Through this family, God was giving us triple the amount of space, for the exact same price that we were currently paying for our apartment. My wife and I shouted and celebrated as we could not believe what was taking place. God is indeed extremely faithful, and when you trust Him and seek first the Kingdom of God and His righteousness, He is more than able to take care of your needs as well as to give you the desires of your heart. We thanked both him and his wife for their gracious kindness, and shared with them both how much of a blessing they were to our family.

A little while later, I received a call from the gentleman to finalize our family moving into their home. During that call, the gentleman began to share with me that God was still dealing with him concerning our family. After encouraging me, he told me that instead of giving them the full amount of what we were currently paying monthly for our apartment, he told me that for an entire year we would only have to pay them five hundred dollars a month for their home, and that they were going to cover and take care of all of our utility costs in full.

Sometimes you can get so use to going without, that you really don't know how to respond when blessings start coming into your life. The only thing that my wife and I could do was cry for joy. For them to make that kind of a sacrifice made a very significant difference in the amount that we would have to pay out monthly. We felt completely overwhelmed by the blessings of the Lord. My family and I had been through so much, and we had been living without for so long, that this moment seemed to be completely unreal to us.

We repacked all of our things, got through the three flights of steps at the apartment complex, and moved into our new home getting our family settled once again. After getting things situated, my wife and I began to just thank God for His blessings and His provision. It was such an amazing moment and such an amazing time for our family. We had finally moved to the city of Battle Creek, and we were blessed with a beautiful place that we could call home.

A few weeks later, the gentleman called me to check and see how we were adjusting to the new place. I told him that we were adjusting well and that it was indeed a blessing. I let him know that we were extremely grateful for all that he and his wife had done for us. He told me that he was glad to hear that our family was adjusting well. He then said to me that God was still dealing with him concerning our family. In that conversation, he told me not to worry at all about paying anything for rent. He said that him and his wife will cover the full cost of our rent and that they will also cover all of our utility expenses for an entire year. He told me not to focus or to worry about that area of my life, but to focus on the ministry that God was calling me to do.

Now I don't know if that gentleman had ever heard a grown man cry on the phone like that before, but that was such an intense moment for me. For a long time my family and I struggled and went without for many years suffering silently. No one, absolutely no one knew the behind the scenes journey that my family and I had to endure... including this family. They didn't know then, and even up to the point that this book has been written and released, we still never shared our personal journey with them. I say this only because I want it to be emphatically clear, that this family did not pour into us out of sympathy for what we had gone through. They truly followed the leading of the spirit, and their kindness impacted our family in such a powerful and an unforgettable way.

The journey that we had to face was painful and filled with so many different levels of uncertainty. Yet through God's grace we continued to push, press, and pursue after our destiny even though every obstacle we had ever faced was screaming at us to give up and throw in the towel. Now that we had persevered through the storm, God had now blessed us with exceeding, abundantly, above all that we could ask or even think.

When you're dropped and left in the middle of the ocean, sometimes you get tired of seeing water, you get tired of swimming. Your arms and your legs get weak from just trying to stay afloat. You become scared of the waves developing around you, you become fearful of what could be lurking beneath you. Your mind even starts to work against you as you look around to see that there is no glimpse of shoreline or land in sight. But when God finally rescues you and brings you to safety, there is such a greater level of appreciation for a God who loves you enough, not to let you drown. I have found this fact to be true in my life both naturally and even spiritually. The hymn writer James Rowe penned it best when he wrote these words, *I was sinking deep in sin, far from the peaceful shore, very sinking stained within, sinking to rise no more, but the master of the sea heard my despairing cry, and from the waters lifted me, now safe am I,* it was truly God's love that lifted me.

Sink Or Swim

CHAPTER NINE

SURVIVOR'S BY FAITH

As I now look over the congregation that God has blessed me to pastor, I am so amazed. There are Doctors, school Principals, teachers, community leaders, successful business entrepreneurs, semi professional basketball players, ex-thugs, ex-gangsters, former drug-dealers, former pimps, former prostitutes who all have one thing in common, they all love Jesus. When I come into our church every week and see such an amazing diversity and beautiful mix of people radically worshiping God with such freedom, as well as watching them grow in their faith, it always reminds my wife and I that the sacrifices that we had to make to bring this ministry to pass was worth it all. It was worth all of the pain, sweat, and tears that we cried many nights on each other's shoulders. It was worth the long and vigorously exhausting road trips of traveling back and forth between two cities for several years, often times borrowing my father's car because our car could not make the road trip. It was worth the many hospital visits that had me laying on a hospital bed in the E.R. unit sometimes at very late hours of the night wondering if I would even make it through my situation. It was worth sitting on the floor of our children's room, holding back our tears as we packed up our boys clothes and toys into boxes because we were losing our home. Someone may wonder how I could say such a thing. I can say those things with full confidence because it was in those very painful places where my family and I discovered God the most. Nothing allows you to discover the multi-faceted levels of God's divine character like trouble itself. And throughout our journey, my family and I discovered attributes of God at a level that often times we had only heard others speak about. God was no longer just a deliver, but He became our deliver. He was no longer just a provider, but He had become our provider. And now having gone through such an incredibly unpredictable journey, the mere thought of God's love and His protection toward us, truly takes on a whole new meaning for my family and I.

I am sure that there are some people that have read through this book, and there are others who will possibly hear about our journey who may take on the final conclusion that the experiences we went through, accompanied with the blessings that we received, were all merely by coincidence and happen stance. But for me, there is no way that coincidence could have navigated such a faith-filled expedition as this. There are way too many divine intervening moments that happened precisely at the right exact times. This fact alone has given me the confident assurance that God was at the forefront of our entire journey. If that however was not enough proof, while I was recently in prayer, God began to take me back throughout the course of our entire journey. There were so many areas in which God removed the backdrop curtain of our life, revealing to me the behind the scenes of how He had been right there for our family the entire time - especially in our most difficult and our most challenging moments when it felt like He was nowhere to be found.

As God began taking me back throughout our journey, I felt God empress within my Spirit a question. He asked me, "do you remember when you were about to lose your house?" I said, "yes Lord." He said, "...and do you remember when you were serving the church with everything that you had, but you still had to go and get a job to try and keep your home?" I told Him, "yes Lord, I remember." He then asked me, "...do you remember the name of the company that you worked for?" I had to stop and think about it for a moment as it had been such a long time since I had worked there, but after I remembered, I went into total amazement. Out of all the places that I could have worked for in the city of Grand Rapids Michigan at that moment in my life, through a temp agency I worked for a company called S.O.S. Office Supply. The abbreviation of Sink or Swim is S.O.S., and I worked there in a season right before those words had been spoken to us. Not only is S.O.S. the abbreviation for Sink or Swim, but the terminology "S.O.S." is an international distress signal that is used when ships are in severe trouble in the ocean or at sea. It is a call and a desperation cry for immediate assistance. It is a declaration that we can no longer handle this situation on our own, and that we are desperately in need of urgent help right away or we will sink. And right before we had embraced the hardest obstacles of our lives, it was as if though God was purposely giving us a sign (that we would only be able to detect later on in our future) to let us know that He had indeed been right there with us the ENTIRE TIME - and that help had already been sent out long before we had ever even known of what boisterous storms and out of control winds and waves we would have to face in our soon coming future.

It is moments like these, that as I began to journal and read back throughout the course of our journey, and seeing God undoubtedly with us the entire way, that I realized clearly that I could not keep our journey to ourselves. The main focal point of what is written in these pages is not intended to be on what we went through, but rather to be focused on the one who brought us out. God is well able to keep you through whatever situations you may ever face in life, and He has a proven track record of protecting and keeping those who truly believe in Him, serve Him, and love Him.

So as you go through your personal journey, don't be discouraged. The bible encourages us to trust in the Lord with all of our heart and to lean not unto our own understanding. It is because our understanding is limited and can be flawed by a shorter view of a larger journey. We have a tendency to respond to things based upon what seems best for us at the moment, rather than to respond to things based upon what God may desire for us. Often times it is because we want immediate relief, and we will naturally and most commonly pick the road of least resistance. Whatever can stop the pain the quickest, whatever can take away the hurt of being abandoned, whatever can elevate the frustration of being rejected or feeling unloved, alone or unwanted; whatever can bring in some quick revenue because of desperate times. All of these thoughts tend to be the way the human heart and mind often gages painful situations. But if you learn how to trust in the Lord with all of your heart and lean not to your own understanding, if you learn how to trust in the one who is right now already working behind the scenes of your life, when you acknowledge Him in all your ways and allow Him to guide you through your storms, the bible says that He will direct your path. Now He may not necessarily direct you away from the storms as you may prefer Him to, but God is well able to skillfully, creatively, and masterfully take you through each and every storm, while keeping you safe until you finally reach your destined place of purpose.

God keeping His people during raging storms (especially while in the presence of large bodies of water) is nothing new in the bible. Whether it's through the story of Moses and God's people who were trapped between their enemies and the Red Sea, or perhaps the story of Jonah who was thrown into the sea itself, but was preserved and kept alive while still in the same water that he was actually thrown into.

Out of them all, there is a story in the bible that deals with a storm that seems to stand out to me from the rest. It is the account of Jesus, who while at sea with His disciples was hit with a very brutally violent and raging storm. The waves were completely out of control, water was pouring into the boat fast and all of the disciples were absolutely frantic. As you read the story in the bible, you can feel the adrenalin racing through the disciples as they were completely overwhelmed by this moment. They had been in storms before, but this one.... this one seemed to be way too much for them to be able to survive through. This was it. It was now clear and evident that nothing more could be done. The ship was taking in way to much water, and the winds and waves were vigorously out of control. That night, every person who was on board that ship knew that this was the end and that they were soon about to perish. The boat that had held them afloat all the way up to this moment of their journey, was now sinking and would soon be lost in the middle of the turbulent sea. In an effort to try and stay alive, while being a very long distance from the shore, these men would only have one of two options, they could either sink or swim.

Through all of this turmoil.... where was Jesus? Where was He at during all of this chaos. Truthfully, it was Jesus fault that they were even out there in that deadly storm in the first place. He was the one that had told them to travel across the sea that night, and now the man who was responsible for all of this was now nowhere to be found. When Jesus was finally discovered, the bible says that He was located in the hinder part of the ship sleeping on a pillow. Not only was Jesus sleeping through this storm, but He was comfortable while He was doing it. When they woke

Jesus up from His rest, extremely disheartened, upset, troubled, and I'm sure a bit disturbed that Jesus could actually sleep peaceably through all of this, they asked Him a question that I believe most of us tend to ask God when we feel like we are about to drown in an unnecessary storm. They asked Jesus, don't you care that we perish? In other words, everything around us is falling apart, we have tried everything that we could possibly do to save this ship, and there is nothing else that can be done. This storm without any doubt is going to kill us, and don't you even care that we are all about to perish and die here?

How many times have you asked God that same question... Do you even care about what I'm going through? How many times have you felt like these men on this sinking boat did during this very life threatening moment. The disciples emotions were everywhere, they were upset, they were mad and frustrated, they were hurt and even scared. They were going down fast with no solutions in sight.

I want to take my final moments with you in this book, to encourage all of you who may really be struggling through some hard pressing issues of life. Some of you are in the middle of a Sink or Swim situation yourself, and it looks and feels like you are soon to drown in what you are going through. You may have tried everything that you can do to stay afloat, but the water of your situation may be coming in your boat faster than you can get it out. I know we felt that way many times. I cannot even begin to share with you how often my wife and I looked at each other and said to ourselves, "this is it, there is no way that we will be able to survive through this." But what is so amazing to know and what is so important for us all to remember, is the fact that even our most fierce, overwhelming and out of control storms that we will ever face in life, must obey God.

Jesus get's up, and the bible says that He speaks directly to the wind and to the sea. He says to them both "Peace, be still," and the bible says that the wind ceased and that there was a great calm that immediately took place. I am wondering what had to be going on in the mind of His disciples who had just watched an extremely intense hurricane-like storm, completely calm itself in just a matter of seconds. Could you imagine the look on their faces as they were trying to figure out what just happened. The disciples final conclusion to what took place is recorded at the very end of the story in Matthew 8:27. It is something that rings out and is a distinct reminder to every believer who will ever find themselves in a sink or swim situation. As the disciples processed and gave their final assessment of what had just taken place, they concluded their assessment with a question. They asked, "*what manner of man is this, that even the wind and the sea obey Him?*"

Raging storms, tempest winds, and violent waves lose their fear crippling grip over your life, when you recognize your with the one who's voice they must obey. When Jesus speaks to your problem, no matter how out of control the situation may be, no matter how unfixable the problem is, no matter how deep you may have begun to sink in your circumstances, at the sound of His voice and at the word of His command your situation must change. How do I know this to be true? My family and I are a living witness. When we knew for a fact that we should have died where we were, God spoke to the heart of our situation and provided life instead of death, success instead of failure, and blessings instead of calamity. And I know for certain that if God did that for us, He is well able to do the same thing for you.

God used that out of control storm to teach His disciples how to deal with raging storms in their lives. A few chapters later, the disciples find themselves in yet another storm similar to the one that they had just experienced before, but this time Jesus was not on the boat with them. The bible says that Jesus came walking on the water in the storm. When Peter recognized who Jesus was, He asked Jesus to allow him to come out on the water with Him. Peter's perspective and view of storms had now completely changed. Opposed to him being fearful of what certainly had the power to completely overtake him, he recognized that if he could keep his eyes on Jesus, that he could walk on top of what he was meant to Sink in.

My prayer is that as you have read throughout our story, that it has given you a new perspective of storms. I am hopeful that these pages have somehow birthed within you a new tenacity to endure adversity, a stronger desire to deepen your faith, the courage to trust God more, and the drive to make it to the end of your journey. It is amazing to me that Peter did not ask Jesus to calm the storm first. It would have made everything much easier if Peter was going to attempt to walk out on that water. But instead, right in the middle of chaotic crashing waves, Peter asked the Master of the sea, to let him come out with Him on the water right in the middle of the storm. He knew that if Jesus was there with him in that storm, that he could defy the odds, and not only walk through the storm, but also walk on top of the sea, surviving through what had the potential to take his life. I pray that you will do as Peter did, and not be fearful to step out keeping your eyes on Jesus. Defy the odds, believe God for the impossible, remain calm in the storm, and I am a living witness that God can and will keep you safe until you finally arrive to shore.

I have shared our story in this book to give all glory to God for bringing us through every obstacle that we have ever had to face. Once again I am hopeful that somehow and in some way, what we have experienced and endured through our journey has encouraged you to continue trusting, believing, and striving toward the purpose and the destiny that God has for your life. If you trust God and hold on to Him, He will preserve, protect, and provide for you until you are able to prevail over your Sink or Swim situation. Don't give up now, there are too many people who are waiting and are in need of YOUR testimony. I thank you for taking the time to read ours, but now it's time for you to live out yours!

I want to conclude this book by leaving you with an encouraging word that I received from a very unusual place. Of all places to receive a word of encouragement, it actually came from the movie Finding Nemo. One day I found myself watching this movie with my three young boys, and the movie came to a scene were Dory the fish began to encourage Marlin (Nemo's father) after he had become fearful of having to go to a deeper and much darker place in their journey. Dory started to sing a tune that not only got stuck in Marlin's head in the movie, but somehow, it also got stuck in mine as well. All she kept singing was, *"just keep swimming."* As you get ready to put this book down, and as you prepare to deal with the real waves of life in your Sink or Swim situation, realize that you didn't come this far to die here, whatever you do... just keep swimming and believing God, and He will come through for you. And soon by faith, like Peter, as long as you keep your eyes on Jesus, you can even walk on top of situations and circumstances that had the potential to cause you to sink.

Dear God,

I thank you for every person who is reading this prayer that has not given up, but may feel like giving up in their Sink or Swim situation. I pray that you would strengthen them, encourage them, and that you would reveal yourself to them like you have done so many times for my family and I. I send out an ***S.O.S.*** *"Spiritual emergency distress call" on their behalf. Send your angels to protect and keep them through their most challenging times. Turn their tears of discouragement into tears of determination. Encourage their heart and give them the courage to keep fighting, the strength to keep on going and the mind to keep believing. Let them see clearly, that what is at the end of this journey is worth making it through every painful moment. Let them have a tenacity and a drive like Peter, to not hide in the boat from their storms, but to realize that with you they can truly survive through every circumstance that is raging around them. If my family and I could make it through with you, then without any shadow of a doubt, they can make it too. I pray this all in Jesus name, amen.*

Sink Or Swim

CHAPTER TEN

ENCOURAGEMENT FOR PASTORS

Bonus Chapter

I want to take a moment to stop and personally encourage all Pastors who truly have a heart after God and also have a genuine heart for God's people, who may be going through some very hard pressing moments right now in life. Just recently, there have been several Pastors and yes even a report of a First Lady who unfortunately has taken their life. It is always painfully devastating and very tragic to hear when such a loss takes place within the body of Christ. Many people really do not recognize the strain and the stress that can come along with being in such a position, and truthfully speaking, the stress and strain of the church can not only affect the Pastor and the First Lady, but it can also affect the entire First Family, including their children. From living at the church with their parents because of meetings and activities, to sometimes hardly seeing their parents because of ministry related events, to the strong and great expectations that may be placed on them for being a Pastor's child, to also the negative dogma that can tend to be placed over them for just simply being known as what has affectionately been labeled as a "PK" (meaning Pastor's Kid). The stress of having this position is something that can truly affect the entire family.

To Pastor over a congregation can bring about so many different levels of personal challenges in a Pastors life, and often times those challenges are fought and dealt with behind the scenes. Many Pastors are very gifted motivators and incredible encouragers for so many others, but honestly, behind the scenes many of those great leaders suffer silently.

There are so many varying circumstances that can cause deep levels of stress, anxiety, depression, frustration, hurt, fear, anger, and so much more in the heart of a Pastor. Those things can be very crippling, however one of the most challenging things to deal with while wrestling with all of those other problems, is something called loneliness. It can be dreadfully painful to feel like you don't have anyone that you can talk to, or to feel as if though you don't have the personal support that you may need. Sometimes that lack of support is not always from just receiving outside help, but sometimes the lack of support can come from actually within your own congregation. It can become frustrating trying to bring a vision to pass that you know God has given you, while you lack the committed support of people within your own congregation who are willing and dedicated to help you bring it to pass. This is not only a problem that occurs within smaller churches, but it is a problem that also occurs in larger congregations as well. In fact, it can become even more devastating to go through a situation like this with a larger congregation, because you know that you have the people needed to make the vision work, but unfortunately only a hand full of those people may actually commit themselves to helping you execute the vision.

It is situations like these that if one is not careful, it can bring about great levels of unhealthy pressure and intense levels of stress. It is because now those Pastors not only feel as if though they don't have the outside support or help that they may need, but they also feel as if though they lack the much needed help and support from within their own congregations. This can lead Pastors down a very isolated and painful road of loneliness.

I have not even begun to talk about the many Pastors who deal with personal struggles, as pastors are human too. We are all tested and tempted, we all get frustrated from time to time. There are times when we get mad and upset like anyone else does. Many times Pastor's are in need of that same forgiving blood of Jesus that we offer to our congregations, yet often times that grace of being properly and truly redeemed and properly restored seems to only be acceptable for everyone else besides the Pastor themselves. There are many Pastors who courageously and unselfishly stand in the gap on the frontline of this very spiritual battle for their church and for their members, all the while suffering and in great need of personal help, encouragement, healthy godly counsel, and strength for themselves. The majority of them feeling as if though they have absolutely nowhere to go, or no one that they can turn to.

I could go on and on listing so many varying circumstances and situations that many Pastors face, but I want to take this moment to stop and encourage every Pastor who may be reading these pages. The first thing that I want you to know is that you are not in this by yourself. There are so many Pastors who are going through the same exact struggles that you are facing right now. Your situation is not at all unique or an isolated circumstance. There is a high percentage of Pastors who wrestle with the thought of calling it quits. Some who wrestle with giving up on their church or giving up on their vision and unfortunately, as it has recently been revealed through the very recent tragic events, there are some who even wrestle with giving up on life. You are not the only one who has struggled or even struggles with these thoughts and circumstances. There are many other Pastors who deal with these painful issues.

What you also need to know is that there are many Pastor's who have also conquered those same thoughts and those same circumstances, and have continued to press and push through them, until they were able to stand in victory. Why is that so significant and important for you to know? Because it proves that it is possible to gain the victory over what you are going through right now. One of the deceptive lies of the enemy is to try and make us feel, think, and believe that what we are going through will always be this way, and that it will never change. He tries to distract us as Pastors in getting so focused on the painful situations that we are going through, that we begin to take our focus off of God. And honestly, if you

171

place your focus on your problems long enough, you may even find yourself getting upset with God. But what we must realize is that those things are being used as a distractive tactic, to pull you away from the very one who can not only give you the strength to endure your problems, but who also has the power to completely bring you out of it and turn your situation around.

I encourage you Pastor to rediscover your prayer closet. Take some much needed time to get inside of your personal prayer chamber and just lay before God. There is something powerful that happens when a Pastor humbly lays before God in prayer while their back is against the wall. God truly encourages and strengthens those, who humbly seek after Him in their most hard-pressing and overwhelming circumstances.

There are so many times throughout our journey that I did not have anyone else that I could talk to. There were many times where I felt like giving up on everything, and I do mean "everything." As you have read our story, you have seen clearly that often times the only thing that I could do was lock myself in the basement of my parents home, and just weep before God. There were times when I was in that basement where I couldn't even say a word, all I could do was weep. Tears would be streaming down my face and my mind could not articulate what needed to be said at the moment. I am so thankful for the Holy Spirit that stood in the gap for me, and the Holy Spirit will do the same for you. Romans 8:26 now has a whole new meaning in my life. It says, ... *the Spirit also helpeth our infirmities: for we know not what we should pray for as we ought: but the Spirit itself maketh intercession for us with groanings which cannot be uttered* (KJV). Every single time I would go before God and pour my heart out before Him, somehow and in some way, God would always encourage my spirit. God would send His peace to me in very uncomfortable situations and in very tight places. My prayer is that as you lay before God, that you will feel His peace and His love overcome your life like you have never experienced it before.

Please know that you are **VALUABLE**, you are **IMPORTANT**, you are **SIGNIFICANT**, you are **ANOINTED**, you are **NEEDED**, and you have **GREAT PURPOSE** in the kingdom of God. Do not let discouragement get the victory over your life. You can conquer whatever storms that may be raging around you through God's help. I also want to encourage you not to be afraid to reach out for help. If you are dealing with deep depression and suicidal thoughts, by all means, do not be fearful to reach out to someone to get the help and support that you may need. It may be a friend, a fellow Pastor, or even a Counselor. Whatever you do, find someone that you can connect to and someone that you can trust, because your life is way too valuable, and there are way too many great things that so many others will receive from you surviving this storm. Reaching out for help is not a sign of weakness, it is a sign of courage and strength.

For those of you who are not Pastors but are reading through this section and you attend a church, please make sure that you take the time to value and appreciate your Pastors. Pray for them, encourage them, strengthen them, and celebrate them. It is extremely hard for a Pastor who pours out all that they have every week, to turn around and feel as if though their sacrifices are being taken for granted, or feeling as if though they are not appreciated. Stand behind your Pastor's vision, get on board with the ministry, help by volunteering where there is great need. Become the support system that your Pastor and first family really need in order to bring the vision that God has given them to pass. If they've made some mistakes, don't through them away, pray for them that they will properly be restored. I've said this before, but it merits repeating again, PRAY for your Pastors DAILY, as they are in much need of your prayers continually. You may never know the hidden struggles or the behind the scene problems that they may be facing in their life, but God does, and when you pray, God can strengthen them in those areas whether you know about them or not.

My last and final word to all Pastors who are reading this book is to be encouraged. The assignment is great, but the God you serve is much greater. Stay in God's presence, stay close to Him, live life on your knees, and soon He will come through for you. May God's power, love, forgiveness, restoration, healing, blessings, provision, peace and strength rest upon you, your church, and your entire family. Thank you for your service to the Kingdom of God and to God's people. Great is the reward for those who faithfully **and with the right heart and spirit** labor in God's Kingdom.

Father,

I pray for every Pastor that is reading this prayer. Though they may be very active in ministry, in their heart they may be screaming, "I Quit!" I pray that you would meet them right at the point of their needs. I pray that through you, they will find the strength and the courage to endure and to persevere through every obstacle that they may be facing in life and in their ministry. God I ask that you touch the hidden struggles and minister to the silent frustrations. Touch the broken areas of their life and help them to heal from the wounds and scars of ministry. Let Galatians 6:9 ring in their spirit, that if they are not weary in well doing, they will reap if they faint not. I pray that you would provide them with the resources needed to bring the vision to pass. I also pray that you would touch the hearts of the people who are already a part of their ministry to unify and support the vision, and that you would send in a fresh harvest of laborers in their ministry that are ready to serve and to also carry out your kingdom assignment. God I pray that you would meet the personal needs of their family as you have done for us so many times. I thank you for their service in the Kingdom, and I give you praise for them right now in Jesus name, amen.

Sink Or Swim
NOTES

Chapter Two
RIPPLES OF CONFLICT
1. Elijah calls fire from heaven - I Kings 18:21-40

Chapter Five
CASTAWAY
1. Steal, Kill, and Destroy - John 10:10

Chapter Seven
SHORE IN THE DISTANCE
1. Jacob wrestling with God - Genesis 32:24-30
2. Facing God - Reference
http://www.biblestudytools.com/lexicons/hebrew/kjv/penuwel.html
(accessed January 10, 2014)
3. Joseph coming out of prison - Genesis 41:14
4. You will reap if you faint not - Galatians 6:9

Chapter Eight
THE MASTER OF THE SEA
1. Exceeding, abundantly, above all - Ephesians 3:20

Chapter Nine
SURVIVOR'S BY FAITH
1. The Story of Noah - Genesis 6 & 8
2. The Red Sea - Exodus 14
3. The Disciples in the storm - Mark 4:35-41
4. Peter walks on water - Matthew 14:22-33
5. Trust in the Lord with all your heart - Proverbs 3:5-6